THE ULTIMATE LIFE

A Return to the "Killing Fields"

This is the true story of a young boy's courage to escape the slaughter in the killing fields of Cambodia only to discover a Saviour in America. Despite family tragedy, culture shock, racism, poverty, and a language barrier, Heng Lim proves that with courage, discipline, and faith in God, anything is possible. This book will inspire all.

—Keith Davis, Missions Pastor, First Baptist Church Owasso

You will not want to put this book down when you start reading it. It will change your life.

—Dr. Jack C. Thompson, Evangelist

Unless otherwise specified, all Scriptures are taken from the King James Version of the Holy Bible.

The Ultimate Life: A Return to the "Killing Fields"
© 2013 Dr. Heng Ly Lim

Printed in the United States of America
ISBN 1-933641-53-3

THE ULTIMATE LIFE

A Return to the "Killing Fields"

A glimpse into "the ultimate life" as seen from
the perspective of a survivor of
the Cambodian "Killing Fields" in the 1970s

Dr. Heng L. Lim

*I lovingly dedicate this book to my wonderful mother,
Say Guech Quindt, and to my beautiful wife, Rachel.*

Mother, you are a true survivor. You went through much hardship that would physically and emotionally cripple most people, yet you have remained strong and courageous. You have taught me much in life. Most of your lessons were not by your words, but by your actions. As long as I live, I will never forget this one thing: that true love demands courage.

Rachel Lim, you are an amazing woman. As a little girl growing up in Cambodia, you went through so much hardship. You are my Cinderella. I love you so much. You are so beautiful—one in a million. God must have known that I desperately needed you to complete my life, and that is why He gave you to me. Like my father, I am very blessed with the love of a beautiful woman. Your love for God, for me, for our children, and for others is so extravagant. You are so kind, considerate, thoughtful, diligent, and godly. I am humbled to be your loving husband.

You have taught me so much about love and honor. When we were dirt-poor in the first four years of our marriage, each day you faithfully made sure I had a home-cooked meal. For my lunch, you packed a cloth napkin, silverware, food, and a glass. All four years during dental school you treated me like a king.

I have made many mistakes in our twenty-plus years of marriage, yet you still adore me. For twenty-two years you have prepared breakfast, lunch, and dinner. Most of the time, you even prepare lunch for our staff. Rachel, you are truly amazing. You have done so many wonderful things for me. No words can describe it all. Thank you for your unconditional love for me. Thank you for being my wife. Not only have you enriched me, you enrich everybody you come in contact with. My mother truly has treasured you as her precious daughter. You are more priceless than any precious stone. I adore you. Your love for me is sweeter than honey.

Table of Contents

Acknowledgements

Many wonderful people have contributed much to this book. I would like to thank Wally Thrun, Jerri Williams, Joyce Ward, and Christi Killian for their contribution in thought, time, and advice. Also I would like to thank Dr. Noah W. Hutchings for his support by publishing this book. Last but not least, I thank my family for supporting me in every step of the book. From the bottom of my heart, thank you. Thank you Christi Killian for beautifully designing the cover and for putting the book together.

Preface

This book is about the life of Dr. Heng Lim, who as a teenager was caught in one of the most severe human tragedies of the twentieth century. The Khmer Rouge (Red Cambodian revolution) in the 1970s drove the Cambodian families into the "killing fields" where fifty percent of the Cambodian population was killed. Young Heng was sent through the jungles to find a way for his family to escape into Thailand. Dr. Heng and his surviving family members, and thousands of other Cambodians, came to the United States where they could begin a new life in freedom. Dr. Heng, still a teenager, went to work at a Christian mission organization where he accepted Jesus Christ as his Saviour. He later became one of the better dental surgeons in the United States. This is a fascinating story of triumph over fear, persecution, and hatred.

—Dr. Noah Hutchings
President, Southwest Radio Church

Foreword

From Boys To Men

Living a Life of Revenge to a Life of Hope

When boys become men, the customary generational process is often structured by the forefathers of each "people group" symbolizing a transition from childhood into adulthood. Knighthood happens after a series of challenges/tests of skills/craftsmanship are met. Native tribes require sons to go through symbolic "rites of passages" to equip their young braves for battle, marriage, and beyond. These symbolic rituals vary and evolve, with some moving toward an ultimate coronation and celebration of life. No matter what nationality you are, the steps to becoming a man require degrees of maturity, discipline, and knowledge. From boy to man is never an "easy" process and it was never intended to be smooth sailing; it might even include sacrifice. From 1965 to 1975, childhood in Cambodia changed dramatically.

What happens to a little boy that grows up in Cambodia during a civil war? What happens when a young boy begins to witness starvation, people being put to death, stealing for food, and trying to catch snakes in the jungle for meals? What happens to a little boy when a communist leader overtakes his family's village and imprisons his family? What happens to a little boy who sees his first execution by a guerrilla warrior openly killing another human with an axe in front of his eyes. The loss of innocence is debilitating. The emotional and spiritual devastation goes off like a nuclear bomb inside the brain, literally tearing at morality and leaving little hope as to a normal future.

A small child growing up with his brothers was about to experience all the horror you could imagine in a span of only ten years. Three of his eight family members would not make it through the horror. They would all grow up facing dangerous trials of fire, reptiles, bandits, imprisonment, abuse, starvation, disease, and killing in jungles where children could not survive alone. These lands, where the *Killing Fields* movie would later be made, ushered in a holocaust that would leave so many millions dead.

Dr. Heng Lim grew up in Cambodia during a holocaust which swept the nation and literally wiped out every living person in his own home village. Yes, this was comparable to those who have endured the worst dictators' rule during wartimes. The wars came in into his neighborhood and then, into his very home. Through the most incredulous of circumstances, his bravery and ability to navigate through hostile territory helped him to successfully escape.

Even when he made it safely to Thailand, he knew he would have to return for his family, literally retracing his own steps through mine fields and pools of dead flesh. He not only memorized his steps, he saved the lives of his mother and three brothers by going five times through the same dangerous trails. This didn't happen without a fight, without battles being lost, without the death of his own father.

He was a small child who would find the only hope for his family was to reach safety in another land. This did not happen, without great sacrifice, death, and traumatic losses. For the first time, I was about to learn of this "journey." Not in a million years was I prepared to hear what I heard. I would never be the same again after our first memorable breakfast.

Everything started with Keith Davis, a young man whom I had mentored two decades earlier and who was currently serving on staff at First Baptist Church of Owasso, Oklahoma. Keith had called me about a "unique story" he felt I needed to hear, knowing filmmakers are often looking for stories. It would be the first time I had even heard from him for the past twenty years. Keith had been following my filmmaking career and he was destiny-driven for me to hear about his friend's life, as he had been serving with Chris Wall, the senior pastor at First Baptist Church, Owasso, and a former dear friend. Chris had come from my home church at Council Road Baptist, where he had served as youth pastor and mentored both of my sons, Michael and Matthew, into the ministry.

We reminisced over the phone about when Keith was called into "special service" when I was serving on staff at Council Road Baptist Church in Oklahoma City two decades earlier. As happens so often in life, Keith and I had just lost touch. He scheduled an appointment with me to bring his "friend" to the city and meet with me over breakfast. Knowing Keith was informed of our past films, *Beyond the Gates of Splendor* and *End of the Spear* about the five men who were speared in the jungles of Ecuador, he knew that we had some background in "telling stories," especially from jungles around the world.

What was interesting was the fact that Keith didn't know we had just returned from Rwanda, Africa, where our film team had been working on a feature documentary film about the 1994 genocide.

We decided to meet at Jimmy's Egg in northwest Oklahoma City one morning and talk about the story Dr. Heng Lim had first written about in *My Journey To Paradise*. Never in my wildest dreams would I believe I could be so completely drawn in to this story, humbly shared, when this courageous man began to open up, sharing the stories of his childhood, the terror he had experienced firsthand, and the miracles that surrounded his journey.

I could not help but stare at the title from the book he handed me. In red letters one specific word jumped off the pages for me, it was the word "journey."

My mind flashed back to a luncheon that a dear friend, Gigi Graham, had set up for me several years earlier with her father, Dr. Billy Graham. Gigi and I had been friends for many years, and this was such an honor to get to spend time with one of the greatest evangelists who had ever lived (at the time he was ninety-one years of age). Anytime you get in front of an incredibly wise man, you have to carefully ask the right questions, so I took the opportunity to ask for his advice regarding filmmaking and the one question in my mind was, "Dr. Graham, if you were a filmmaker today, what kind of movies would you be making?"

I will never forget his humble words to me after a long pause: "Let me think on that, Kevin." My heart sank somewhat because I was really seeking his noble insight, godly wisdom, and support. When would he give me his thoughts, if not then? Maybe the question was wrong, so I politely said thank you, not knowing if an answer would ever come.

About an hour later, Dr. Graham's pastor from Greenville walked in the door at Piney Cove where he has lived for many years. His pastor was originally from South Africa and Dr. Graham said to both of us, "Don, I want you to meet Kevin McAfee, as he is a filmmaker and makes great movies and he asked me a question and I really want to know what you think." Isn't it like a great man to honor his pastor? I loved that about what I was experiencing.

Pastor Don Wilhoite shared his words of wisdom for me, how to pray for insight and more. Truly, it was a divine appointment that meant a lot to me. Later, we would get to hug each other's neck again at Gigi and Jimmy's wedding, an incredible reunion love of many decades!

Then as if on cue from Heaven, Dr. Graham turned to me, placed his hand on mine, and said, "Kevin you should make movies about a journey. People's journey are where their stories can impact the world." Pastor Don agreed, and Gigi smiled and nodded affirmation. When I left there, I found myself so energized looking for a journey. Seeking a story about a powerful journey led me to our meeting.

It was as if prophetically, Dr. Graham had told me the "key word" to look for in the story—the word for today was "journey." This was a very real answer to my own prayer, *My Journey to Paradise* from Dr. Heng Lim, a biographical trail that had been paved by a man who had been radically transformed.

As a filmmaker, I've made several movies about "journeys" when death was at the pinnacle of the story. We had spent time in South America learning of the Waodani killings in Ecuador, and I thought to myself that we may have already covered this topic before. Even the terror imposed from the 1994 genocide in Rwanda had broken my heart during the shooting of our film *Through the Valley,* which I had just directed and produced. What we also learned from filming *The Samaritan* with Colonel Oliver North had similar communist overtones. In 2006 I had directed a documentary feature about an attorney named Edward Roush who overcame huge odds to free a family from tyranny. It was about a communist dictator who had killed over two million people of faith, even bulldozing churches. Death had become very real.

Heng's story would be totally different because it was looking at the world of death and tragedy through the eyes of a revenge-oriented child. Why was I being led to another story where slaughter was a way of life? How could a small boy's journey be different, and what lessons could really be learned? One reason: this was a journey unlike any other I had ever known.

At Jimmy's Egg, across from our omelets and pancakes, I sat there in amazement after fifteen minutes of listening to Dr. Lim share his story. I found myself literally weeping with him. Dr. Lim sat next to Keith, who was crying as well, and he shared openly the most dramatic story of any childhood I had ever heard in my life. The incredible moments that he endured from six to sixteen years of age were indeed crippling emotional hurdles that robbed children of their childhood, leaving most on a trail to prison or death.

I knew if nothing ever came from this meeting, I needed to know more of the bravery that Heng had lived and that his story might reveal. We talked more about what happened, why he was going through this, how his family survived, and what the greatest obstacles he could share were.

Here was a young boy, the son of a butcher, living in the province of Tekvil, twenty miles south of Phnom Penh, the capital of Cambodia, who was so filled with hatred, the only thing he could focus on was revenge. After everything he had endured, he was seeking answers, but the answers were not there. He became angry—angry at everything—and it was natural for him to hate, to want to kill and destroy everything in his path. When you live a life where you begin to question if there is a God because of everything cruel that surrounds you, how can you possibly find answers? What was unbelievable was that we were sitting across from a man who had the kindest eyes, the most sincere smile, and the humblest of natures. What kind of miraculous transformation had taken place that would change his heart?

After the meeting, we were all emotionally exhausted because it lasted several hours. There was no doubt; I knew we needed to learn more about his story, so we scheduled a meeting with our families in his hometown. It was important we talk to Rachel, his wife, and get more of an understanding of what happened to him and learn how their lives had intersected, since she was Cambodian as well. From the initial meeting, we found out that when he came to the United States at sixteen, he was basically illiterate.

He got several jobs to help provide for his family, one of which was working at the Southwest Radio Church in production; the other job was sacking groceries. He was surrounded by the Catholic Church, the Episcopalian Church, and the Baptist Church all offering to help him, sponsor his family, and provide opportunities in this new place called America. As a refugee from Cambodia, he would quickly learn of the love of people in the faith community. He went to one of the largest church camps in the world. It was there with the campers from Northwest Baptist Church during a worship service where he sang in the choir, that his life changed forever after making a spiritual decision to follow the Christ of Christianity.

Going to school he overcame all obstacles, became a doctor of dentistry, and now has one of the most prominent practices in the Southwest, where people come from all over the world for a perfect smile. Doors began to open for him to speak and he shared of his life in front of organizations, churches, and beyond. His story of rags to riches is one of the great stories of hope we all have come to understand. The next series of meetings would even be more astounding as we traveled to the northeastern side of the state to Owasso to meet his family.

When we met with Rachel, Heng's wife, we found that they had met serendipitously at a college conference in Missouri. What was even more amazing was that they grew up just a few miles away from each other in Cambodia and were deported within months of each other from the same refugee camp. Their lives would both be filled with torment and terror that no child should ever experience.

In fact, Rachel would be beaten almost to death in one of her captivities where she miraculously escaped. Together, this incredible couple now journeys to many countries with a powerful message of hope, of deliverance, and of a new future embedded in their own faith. They are driven to share the gospel, to reach out to orphans and widows, and to do everything they can to bring jobs to Cambodia and to the utmost parts of the world.

Veritas Entertainment is our film company, and we are producing a feature length documentary called *Journey to Paradise;* it will be about the life of Heng and his wife Rachel, where they tell their own true stories of their unbelievable journeys in Cambodia and beyond. After completing this documentary feature and sharing this with faith groups all over America and around the world, a narrative feature film will be created to highlight their childhood stories.

I would highly recommend you read *My Journey to Paradise* by Dr. Heng Lim first and then immerse yourself in this new book Dr. Lim has written, *The Ultimate Life: The Return to the Killing Fields.*

It is the postlude to a symphonic life's work that reveals how a small child grew to be a man in minutes. A story of hope, of forgiveness, and of transformation where a young man under a tree cried out to God, and God heard his cry and delivered him. An epic story of biblical proportions where, with miracle after miracle, this little jungle boy grew to become a man unlike most men you will ever meet in your life.

It is my honor, and with utmost respect, I introduce you to my new friend, Dr. Heng Lim, one of the bravest men I have ever known. His story will stand for the hundreds of thousands that did not make it out of the killing fields, to the families and friends he personally lost, and to his wife's family and friends who were miraculously rescued from hopelessness.

This is his journey . . .

In Veritas,

Kevin D. McAfee
Founder/Filmmaker
Veritas Entertainment

Chapter 1

The Killing Fields

The year was 1976, and the place was by a creek next to our home underneath the shade of a cottonwood tree. It was a very desperate and dark time—we were living under the dictatorship of the ruthless Khmer Rouge regime. The communists were forcing us at gun point to work in extreme conditions out in the rice field. We weren't allowed much food. We were very sick and we were starving. Father was dying. He looked like a skeleton. He was filthy, covered in his own urine and feces, and his stench was foul. Yet mother cradled him and loved him unconditionally.

As his last wish before he died, father craved a taste of sweetness on his tongue. Everyone knew that the only person in the village who had any sugar was Comrade Hai, nicknamed "The Killing Machine." He was so wicked that no one looked into his eyes and lived. Mother knew that this monster had killed hundreds of people in the village; he had hung their gallbladders as his trophies. Nevertheless, she courageously went to face him. Anxiously, we waited for her return, not knowing if she was going to live or die. She hurried back with a little jar of palm sugar to feed him. Father may have died from a lack of food, but his heart was surely full of love.

Once, long ago, in a land far away, there lived a young, noble king in a kingdom across the great sea. The people of his kingdom loved him deeply, and were extremely devoted to him. Even though the king was very young, he reigned over his beautiful kingdom with great dignity, making sure that his people were living in peace and prosperity. The people were very happy . . . until the darkest day of a deeply troubled time arrived.

On that day, a dark, evil force descended from the north, sweeping down into the empire to the east of the kingdom of the young king. This force bewitched the minds of the people into believing that their rulers weren't being fair to them. It led them to believe that they were being mistreated and abused.

The dark force cast its spell into peoples' hearts and tricked them into believing that everyone in the empire should have equal status and be free from any form of rule. It bewitched them with the idea that they were entitled to have an "ultimate life," living in a utopian community here on earth. The only change they would have to make was to overthrow their government.

Sadly, people believed the dark force.

The dark force swiftly split the eastern empire in half, dividing it into a northern kingdom and a southern kingdom. The people of these two kingdoms looked alike—they all had black hair and yellow skin, but some of the northern kingdom people had black teeth from chewing a special kind of nut.

Like a wild, consuming fire, the dark force relentlessly attacked the southern kingdom. In their defeat and despair, the southern people cried out for help from another king who ruled a powerful and prosperous kingdom flowing with milk and honey. This powerful king was very big and tall, his skin was white, and his hair was grey.

Knowing that the dark force could spread its tentacles into the surrounding kingdoms, the white king became extremely disturbed. Quickly, he sent thousands of his warriors by air and by sea to defend the southern kingdom. The white king's warriors went to the battlefields, some flying in the bellies of big steel birds with silver wings, and some riding on iron battleships that could spit fiery cannonballs like a dragon. *The big steel birds could drop large exploding eggs, their blazing thunder killing people and leaving behind craters as big as giant ponds. The white king's warriors bravely fought against the dark force's army. They successfully won the battle and pushed the dark force back up to the north.*

But the dark force was wickedly cunning. It moved its forces westward into the dense forest of the young king's lands. The dark force used this thick forest as its hiding place, a safe haven where it could sneak its attacks on the white king's warriors in the southern kingdom. The dark force injured and killed many of the white king's warriors.

This made the white king very angry. He sent his royal messenger to warn the young king, "Close the border of your kingdom from the dark, evil force!" But the young king didn't receive the warning kindly, and so he did not cooperate with the white king.

Meanwhile, in the kingdom of the young king there arose an evil man named Salath Sar. The dark force had also entered his heart. He became very discontented with the way the young king was ruling over the kingdom. Salath Sar believed that his way was better. He went around the country trying to convince peasants and farmers to follow him, and to revolt against the king. He promised people "the ultimate life"—equal distribution of wealth, better opportunities, and "a great leap into the future." He persuaded people to leave their villages and families to join forces with him in the forest. He called his guerilla force the "Khmer Rouge." These guerilla fighters wore black pajamas with red scarves wrapped around their necks as uniforms.

Seeing the great benefits Salath Sar had promised them, many peasants and farmers quickly joined forces with him to attack the young king. Now the young king had two sets of enemies—one outside his kingdom, and another within.

While the young king was out of his kingdom for his royal rest, the white king sent his forces to overthrow the young king. The white king removed him from his throne and placed the young king's most trusted general as ruler in his place.

Attempting to reclaim his throne, the young king and Salath Sar became allies. He then sent out royal messages calling his people to join the existing guerilla force of Salath Sar in the forest. Since most people in the kingdom loved and trusted their king, they left their families and homes to join the guerilla force, and suddenly the small Khmer Rouge force was greatly fortified in strength and numbers.

Back in the kingdom of the white king, people began to complain about the suffering and death of war. They heard news and saw pictures of the brutality of the war. Many of them believed that this war was gravely unjustified, and that their warriors had no right to go across the great sea to kill innocent people in another kingdom. Some even called their brave warriors "baby killers." They protested intensely for their king to bring their warriors back home. They demanded an immediate peace.

Now the white king found himself in the same predicament as the young king. He was fighting two wars, one within his kingdom, and another in a kingdom across the great sea. Out of frustration, the white king reluctantly commanded all his warriors to retreat. With great disappointment, the steel birds with silver wings carried the warriors back home, leaving some behind as prisoners of war. Suddenly, the dark force overtook both the northern and southern kingdoms.

Thus, the communists won the war. In Cambodia, Salath Sar changed his name to Pol Pot and put himself on the throne. The young, noble king did not return to take his throne as he had promised, but instead was deposed into exile in another kingdom. The darkest day of the deeply troubled times had dawned in Cambodia. The month was April, the day was the seventeenth, and the year was 1975.

This is not a fairy tale—it is a true story. I was there when it all happened. I was ten years old when the Khmer Rouge took control of

Cambodia. I remember the day like it was yesterday. Did the people of Cambodia receive the ultimate life as promised, or did they get imprisoned with ultimate suffering and death?

Chapter 2

Peace!

The defining moment everyone in Cambodia was waiting for finally arrived. The bloody civil war came to an abrupt end. For the rich, this moment brought them much anxiety, for they had much to lose. For the poor, this moment brought them great hope, for they were anxiously anticipating the ultimate life—the "Great Leap" promised to them by the Khmer Rouge. Five years of war had plunged the entire country into utter ruin as if a tornado had come through, leaving countless families and dreams in utter desolation. People were sick and tired of war and its carnage. They were ready for peace and a radical change.

On April 17, 1975, Cambodia was "rescued" by the Khmer Rouge. Like plants scorched in a desert and longing for moisture, people had waited for the rain of peace to bring them back to life. My family was among the poor and hopeless. This day was both one of the happiest and one of the saddest days of my life and the lives of many Cambodian people. It was the day that literally changed the destiny of our entire country.

Usually, Cambodians celebrate the New Year on April 13. All the shops, banks, markets, schools, and government offices are closed for three days and nights. Old and young people alike excitedly prepare for the New Year by cleaning their houses, and buying or making traditional clothing and food. It is like Thanksgiving and Christmas combined.

Older people celebrate the New Year by going to the Buddhist temple in their best traditional clothes. My family would bring our best prepared food to give alms to the monk. At the temple, we would meet friends and family. Together we sat on the straw mats, folding our legs, with palms together and raised up to our foreheads, worshipping God. We would listen to the monk in orange robes reciting prayers in Sanskrit, which we couldn't understand. While the older people were involved with spiritual celebrations, young people were much more focused on having fun.

Young people usually celebrated the New Year outside in the temple courtyard with traditional dancing and games. One game we played was "Chhoung." A *chhoung* was a kind of soft ball made of a cloth material such as cotton or silk, with a cloth handle. In their beautiful, colorful dresses, the women would stand in a line about twenty-five feet away, facing a line of men. The man holding the *chhoung* would sing a love song, attempting to court the woman of his choice. When he finished his song, he would toss the *chhoung* toward the woman that he had chosen. The women would scurry, fighting for the *chhoung*. Whichever woman caught it would sing her song back to the man. So the courting continued back and forth, with singing and dancing mixed with music and laughter echoing in the city all day and on into the night.

But this year, it was different. The Buddhist temple was empty. The entire country was bracing for the war to end and for life to begin. Instead of hearing the joyous music and laughter of young people and the "beehives" of Sanskrit prayers, bombs and the sound of guns echoed. Wounded people screamed in agony. The ambulances marked with "Red Cross" on the sides, back, and hood blasted their screeching sirens while carrying injured people to the hospital. The street was left empty, like an old Wild West town ready for a gunfight. People fearfully stayed hidden inside their homes. Bombs exploded like thunder all over the city, shaking the ground under our feet. In the night, exploding bombs lit up the dark sky over and across the rivers like Fourth of July fireworks. At night, the city was ablaze. During the day, hundreds of columns of thick, black smoke curled upward into the darkened sky.

One day a navy boat came to the riverbank next to my home. The sailor that was navigating the boat jumped onto the shore with an anchor rope in his hand. He was in a hurry. He quickly wrapped the rope around a tree and dropped the steel anchor to the ground. He ran up the shore to a little house next to mine. For one excited moment I thought this man was my long lost father coming back for me. Overwhelmed, my heart skipped a beat. I was flooded with joy. For one brief moment, I thought that my dream had finally come true. The last time I had seen my father was three years before when he had been kidnapped by the guerilla fighters.

When the civil war erupted in Cambodia, it displaced people from the countryside who sought refuge in the city. Our family moved into the crowded city along the riverbank. Afterward, my father took his parents to see their home in the country. While they were there, the Khmer Rouge abducted him in the jungle. This broke our hearts, especially our mother's. For months, our mother searched all over the country for her husband. Each day, from dawn to dusk, mother left the house to search for our father. She was relentless. Even after her right foot was crushed in a motorcycle accident, she kept going, looking and searching. We all believed that she had turned every stone, but she could not find him anywhere. She wept enough tears to fill a river. But it didn't matter how hard or how far mother went to search—she couldn't find our father.

Our family became bitter toward the Khmer Rouge. We hated them for taking our father away from us. He was a kind and considerate man, never doing wrong against anybody. He was the type of man that would stop and help strangers on the road. As a little boy, I thought that he was very handsome. He was dark tan, strongly built, and the tallest man in town. He had a gentle face, a very handsome smile, and slightly curly black hair. His character matched his features. He was half Cambodian and half Chinese. His father left China in the early 1900s to seek better opportunities in Cambodia. He married my grandmother, a Cambodian woman, and had many children, my father being the oldest son. My grandparents were wealthy businesspeople in Cambodia. They owned rice mills, a large farm, and a big, white southern-style mansion in the suburbs.

War changed everything.

I was terribly disappointed when the navy officer came closer and I realized he wasn't my father. I recognized him as the son of the elderly lady living next door. In full navy uniform, he had come to take his mother away to safety. I could hear him telling his mother that all of the foreign ambassadors and their affiliates had already left Cambodia by airplane and helicopter. He told his mother to hurry up, to pack, and to take only the most important things with her. The two of them left quickly.

I stood there on the riverbank, watching as the navy captain took his mother away with him. As his ship departed, the wake it left behind disturbed countless swollen corpses floating face down, mingled with trash. The odor of rotting human flesh mixed with raw sewage from the overcrowded city could make any nose wilt. The whole country stank. I thought the whole world was a stinking, rotten corpse floating down the river of war.

My mother, with four little sons, lived for three years on this riverbank in a shack not much bigger than a chicken coop. The shack's roof and walls were made of rusted, folded tin metal. No running water. No electricity. No indoor plumbing. In the summer, it was hot and humid. It was so unbearable that during the day we mostly stayed under the shade of the tree. In this home, our mother lost two of her children. Her only daughter died of an uncontrollable fever at the age of three. Some said that it was meningitis. And one of the twin boys died of starvation. Mother had no milk.

The tin walls and roof amplified the noise of the explosions with a lot of shaking and rattling. After the navy officer left, Mother cooked and packed our food—steamed rice and grilled fish. Three charred stones in the corner of the room were still warm from her cooking. That was our stove. We were waiting for the signal to evacuate the city.

Early the next morning, people went out to the street to join the throng welcoming the Khmer Rouge into the city. My big brother Cheang and I stood among the crowd, cheering, "Peace and Victory!"

Cheang was thirteen, but he looked like a full-grown adult. He was big, tall, and strong. He took after our dad. I was ten, but small. I took after our mom. Excited, we screamed and shouted, bursting with joy like the steam from a locomotive. We stood on tiptoe along the curb watching the parade as the Khmer Rouge entered the capital in army jeeps, tanks, trucks, motorcycles, and on foot. Most of them were teenagers and did not look much older than I was. They all wore black "pajama" uniforms with their pant legs rolled up to their knees. They all wore sandals made from car tires. Red scarves were wrapped around their necks. Loaded AK-47s and belts of ammunition were strapped over their chests and backs. Some soldiers carried the big gun on their shoulders. Female soldiers wore bobbed hair. Male or female, all looked angry, walking forward with their jaws tight and their teeth gritted. None smiled.

More people flooded into the streets like monsoon raindrops to cheer the Khmer Rouge "victory." The soldiers responded by shooting their guns into the air and waving the guns with red flags tied to the barrels. Even soldiers from Lon Nol's army joined the celebratory parade. It was easy to identify them. They wore camouflage uniforms with steel helmets to match their army boots. These two armies had been enemies, fighting like cats and dogs, and now they were cheering together. This was a beautiful sight. I ran to the street and joined in the celebration, shouting, "Victory for the revolutionary Khmer!"

Then I caught myself, realizing that I was cheering for my enemy. These were the people who had kidnapped my father. Suddenly my cheer was replaced with hatred for the Khmer Rouge.

Rumors began to spread all over the street and town.

"Our country is going be changed!"

"Peace is coming."

"The king is coming back to reign."

"Prosperity, equality, and justice are coming!!"

"No more war! We can go back home."

I was so happy. The thought of going back home was so great.

Cheang and I left the street and returned to our shack. Uncle Khun, Mom's brother, was already there with his motorcycle waiting for us. "Where have you two boys been?" he scolded us.

"On the street," Cheang replied.

Since Father was gone, Uncle Khun came to see us often. He was like a surrogate father. Being a law student at the university kept him extremely busy. Mom said that Uncle Khun had an opportunity to go to France to study, but he chose not to leave us behind.

Uncle Khun was both extremely intellectual and kind. By not going to France, he missed the opportunity of a lifetime. Being a graduate student at that time in Cambodia was extremely rare. Most people dropped out of school in the second or third grade. My mother did, and so did Cheang and I.

My uncle looked skinny, like my mother. My mother was slim and beautiful. She wore her hair long. Uncle wore glasses and his eyes were small and squinted. Mother said he got those eyes from over-studying. With khaki pants, a white shirt, and eyeglasses, he looked very studious and smart.

"Don't roam around! We all need to stay together. We don't want to leave anyone behind, do we?" Uncle disciplined us.

Later that morning, two soldiers knocked at our door. When the door was opened, one of them said something extremely peculiar. "Mom, Dad, and comrades, Anka asks that you take your family and leave the city at once. Your family is in danger. The Americans are coming to bomb us. Anka asks that all the people evacuate the city for three days. Once the raid is over, you can return if you choose."

We were totally confused as to why these two soldiers called my mother "Mom" and my uncle "Father." Why did he call us boys "comrades"? And who and what was "Anka"?

The street was jam-packed full with a sea of people. We were all making an exodus into the countryside. After only a few hours, the crowd became very thick, with shoulder rubbing against shoulder. Our family desperately tried to stay as close together as possible.

Uncle Khun walked his motorcycle with Thong, my youngest brother, who was two years old, on the seat. Meng, my seven-year-old brother, walked beside us. He was strong and alert for his age. Mom carried a bag of clothes on her head, while Cheang carried a big bag on his shoulder. I carried pots and pans, and some rice and food.

Rich people and poor people alike carried their children on their backs, shoulders, and hips. Some people carried their belongings in wheelbarrows. One man and woman were pushing an old man on a bed that had wheels under it. Some people carried TVs. I thought that these people had no common sense. What good was a TV in the jungle when they could go hungry? Some people put their loads in a car and pushed it along with the crowd. I had never seen so many people!

Several Khmer Rouge soldiers stood along the street, yelling and urging us to move on: "Get out of the city quickly! Mothers, fathers, brothers, and sisters, the Americans are coming to bomb us!" They caused people to panic, but we couldn't walk any faster. Too crowded, too many children, and too much of a load to carry.

Everyone was scared, expecting big steel birds with silver wings—B-52 bombers—to appear in the air at any time. Everyone was in the open—no trench, no foxhole, no bomb shelter to hide ourselves. We were clearly exposed, like the open field to raindrops. People kept looking up, expecting doom to drop on us from the sky. Our family pushed very hard to get out of the city. By late that evening we had barely made it to the outskirts of the city. We were still in the danger zone. Mom's foot was hurting severely. She couldn't put much pressure on it. We camped alongside the street that night.

At dawn, Uncle Khun pulled back our blanket and whispered, "Get up! Cheang, Heng, and Meng, get up! It is time to go! We need to get going before it is too hot."

Wasting no time, we got up and packed our blankets. We ate no breakfast and didn't brush our teeth. We walked barefoot. During the day, the sun could heat up the surface of the road to a blistering heat. That night I had hardly slept; I was too anxious. I thought about the coming bombs. I thought about going back home to the place of my birth. But, mostly, I thought about my father. I wondered if he was waiting for me. I missed him greatly and hoped that he would be there waiting for us at home.

It didn't bother me very much to walk, but our mother had problems. Her ankle was swollen and she was in great pain. She hopped in agony, holding on to one of us. We moved very slowly. We stopped often to rest along the road. "I can't walk anymore," Mother groaned. She wanted to sit down and rest, but each time she sat down the Khmer Rouge came, forcing us to move on.

Out of nowhere, parting the sea of people, a few large army trucks emerged and stopped beside us. A man jumped out of the driver's seat and onto the road. He cupped his hands around his mouth and shouted at the top of his lungs, "People who are weak, old, or too tired to walk can ride in this truck! Anka will take you to the countryside!"

Being naïve, we trusted him.

There were only a few trucks, but thousands of people. My mother and I hustled to get on one. Mom told Uncle Khun, "We will go home first, and we will send people for you! Take care of the boys!" In no time, the back of the truck was packed with people like sardines in a can, with standing room only. People were sweaty and smelled unwashed. The air was so thick we had to drag it in to breathe. Mother and I stood in the very back, where there was more air. We left our family in the crowd.

"We are close to our home now, son!" Mother spoke to me with excitement. I was wondering if the driver was going to stop for us, but he gave no sign that he was going to stop anywhere soon. People standing next to us in the back of the truck told us that the driver was going to take us as far as he could into the countryside and dump us there, near Vietnam.

Frantic, we wanted to stop the truck. But there was nothing we could do to stop it. It was like riding on a roller coaster; it would stop when it was supposed to stop. We couldn't jump—the truck was moving too fast.

Unexpectedly, the truck made a sudden stop. The driver got out to use the restroom. He came to the back and sternly commanded us, "Nobody leaves! Everybody must stay where you are!"

I jumped down as soon as the driver turned to walk away. I stumbled. I fell flat on my stomach. I scraped my knees and the palms of my hands. Pain shot through me, but I gritted my teeth and bore it. I got up and helped my mother out of the truck. She jumped and did the same thing, falling flat on her stomach. Then the two of us scurried across the street to hide behind the shrubs. We looked around, making sure that no one was watching us, and we sneaked into a house. A man in his late fifties was startled at our appearance, but quickly his face broke into a smile.

"Say Guech?" He was surprised.

"Yes, Uncle Hout! Help me and my son! We need to hide. Someone is chasing after us," Mother begged the old man.

"Quickly, hide in my room and stay there until I come to get you!" He guided us there. We did as instructed, sitting in the corner of his room, out of breath. We waited. And we listened to every sound. No footsteps. We took a deep breath.

"Say Guech! It is safe now. Come out! Whoever is looking for you is not here!" Uncle came and shouted out. We came out from our hiding place. Then Uncle Hout told us the most amazing news. Our father was alive, and he had been there earlier looking for us. I couldn't believe what I had just heard. Joy flooded our hearts like a mighty river. No ocean was deep enough to contain our excitement. The news was such a shock that mother burst into tears.

The good news brought us hope. In her disbelief, she questioned him, "Uncle! Did you just say that my husband is alive and he was here looking for me?"

"Yes, Say Guech! Ngoun Sreng, your husband, is alive!" He emphatically stated that our father was living with my mother's older brother, Uncle Sroy.

Have you ever lost anything that is precious to you? Maybe your health, a family member, a treasure, or even a relationship? You felt so empty and desolate. You have searched everywhere. You have lost all hope. And then, at the least expected time, you find it again. If so, then you know how happy it was. That was how happy Mother and I were.

I could not wait to see my father's face. I longed for his embrace. I couldn't wait to tell my daddy everything. I could not wait to tell my brothers about our daddy. What a great day that was! It was one of the happiest days of my life in the midst of this darkest of times.

Chapter 3

Free at Last!

Narrated by Dr. Frank J. Miranda

In 1984, the movie *The Killing Fields,* produced by Roland Joffé, was released. Starring Sam Waterston as a *New York Times* reporter and Haing S. Ngor as his Cambodian liaison, interpreter, and friend, the movie was a violently vivid portrayal of the civil war in Cambodia during the 1970s that spilled over from the infamous Vietnam conflict. For most people, the film was a gripping and sobering account of the rape of a country and its people. One could not help leaving the theater horrified by the events of that time, and no doubt thankful that the carnage occurred far from home.

For Heng Lim, a senior dental student at the University of Oklahoma College of Dentistry, it was an all-too-chilling piece of reality revisited. He and his family lived the horrific scenes depicted, and endured firsthand the tribulation of that brutal era. His story is one of seemingly unending sorrow culminating in an eventual triumph over tragedy. While now secure in his adopted country, the scars of his childhood still remain. To this day, *The Killing Fields* is the only movie that has ever made him cry.

Heng Ly Lim was born on July 15, 1965, in the Kandal Province of Cambodia, the second of six children. His father, Sreng Sim, was from a well-to-do family and worked as a jack-of-all-trades, including as a butcher, a blacksmith, a mechanic, and a bicycle shop operator. His mother, Say Guech Lim, was a housekeeper.

"For the first five years of my life," Lim recalled, "things were great and I have nothing but good memories. But since my family was half Chinese and half Cambodian, we were not strangers to refugeeism even then. My mother's family had to escape from China during the days of Mao Tse-tung and the new communism. Her father and his family came to Tek Vil, a small village in the Kandal Province of Cambodia, where he became an important man in the village. He was even visited by many of the country's dignitaries. We were very well off at this time—just one big happy family, with my parents, my brothers, and many of my aunts and uncles all living in the same little village."

But the tentacles of the ongoing Vietnam conflict were soon to end the serenity.

Because the North Vietnamese communists were attacking South Vietnam from inside Cambodia's border, the United States began bombing Cambodia in 1969. Within a year, Tek Vil was added to the list of Cambodian villages to feel the onslaught of these bombing raids. As the North Vietnamese started to come into the village, Lim and his family left to join his other grandparents in another village some distance away.

"We walked across the rice fields rather than ride the buses because it was more secure," Lim said. "My mother stayed because she had just given birth to my little sister. During our escape, we ran into a battle between the Khmer Republic [the Cambodian capitalists supported by the Americans] and the Khmer Rouge [literally "red" Cambodian], who were communists, but at the time we viewed them as patriotic countrymen.

"Anyway, we made it to my grandfather's village where my father left me and my two brothers and returned to Tek Vil for my mother and sister. A short time later, we moved to Prek-atang, another village closer to the capital city of Phnom Penh. Here I had my second brush with the war when I saw a neighbor get both legs shot off during another battle between the opposing forces. I remember my family lying flat on the ground in our house, surrounded by rice bags, just waiting for the firing to stop. We eventually moved into Phnom Penh proper, where my father found work as a cart driver."

At the end of 1972, the war was to have a more personal impact on then seven-year-old Lim and his family.

"The Khmer Rouge captured my father," Lim recalled haltingly, "took him into the jungle, and forced him to work for them. My mother was pregnant at the time, so this was particularly hard on her. It was to be more than two years before we found out what happened to my father. Our financial security also had completely disappeared. We were now very poor and had no money to pay the rent. Soon after my father was captured, my mother gave birth to twins, but one died two weeks later. A few months after this, my little sister died from general poor health and malnutrition. She was three years old."

Because the family had no place to stay, Lim's grandparents built a small hut for them where they lived in squalid conditions for the next two years. Lim remembered with some pride that he and his brothers worked very hard to help provide meager support for the family.

"We would get up at five a.m. to sell bread all day, come home, and then go out to sell ice cream until late at night. We also did house and yard chores . . . everything."

In 1975, the Khmer Rouge took over Cambodia. The people thought the war was finally over, that Sihanouk would come back from exile, and that the country would get back on its feet again. But the Khmer Rouge began evacuating Phnom Penh and the surrounding provinces at gunpoint, and forcing the people to go into the countryside on foot. Use of vehicles was not allowed.

"We were walking back to our village of Tek Vil," recalled Lim, "and guess what? We found my father! He was in the village with an ox and a cart! Even though we were still poor, we were happy, and we thought everything would be all right."

Weeks later, they were to find out otherwise.

Lim said, "There was no food to eat and no place to stay. All the banks, the schools, the markets, everything, was closed. Just the buildings were there. The Khmer Rouge began rounding up all the people with education, anyone connected with the old government or with foreigners, anyone with ties to capitalism . . . and they executed them. All others were forced to work in the rice paddies as laborers. We were transferred by train to the western part of Cambodia where we were put in a Buddhist temple. Living conditions were terrible. I was ten years old at the time, and from this point on, my one overriding emotion was fear. Soon after arriving at the temple, I saw a man who had complained about the conditions taken outside and executed before our eyes. And for the next four years, the Khmer Rouge would come at night, take people, question them, and beat them. People just disappeared.

"All the families were split up. The men were taken to one area; women and small children to another area. I was forced to live with orphans and work in the rice fields fourteen to sixteen hours a day. My reward at the end of the day was a bowl of rice soup. And believe me—it wasn't like Campbell's soup! The soup was a cup of rice added to gallons of water. I would eat tadpoles, frogs, and wild vegetables—anything I could find in the fields—just to survive, even though I knew I would be executed if the Khmer Rouge caught me.

"My father starved to death during this first year. So did all of his family. After a year, there were no men left. In 1976, I was just a skeleton. Since I wasn't expected to live, I was shipped back to the village where my mother was staying, taken to a Buddhist temple, and left to die. As far as I remember, anyone who went to that temple didn't come out. I honestly don't know how I survived. My mother told me later that she prepared sacrifices as instructed by the 'evil spirit' inside me, and I lived. Being too sick to work, I just walked around eating snails, rats, centipedes, scorpions, anything, just to get some strength back. Before 1976 was over, all of the men and most of the children had died.

"In 1977 we were shipped to the southwest part of Cambodia, closer to Thailand, where we stayed for the next two years. In 1979, the Khmer Rouge went to war with Vietnam. When the Vietnamese came in, my mother, younger brothers, and I packed up our clothes and followed them. We got caught in more crossfire, and I remember having to lie on a fire anthill for an hour while the two sides shot at each other. I can't remember how many times I must have been stung. But it was better than being shot! I also remember seeing a friend of my mother's literally get blown to bits by a grenade launcher."

With hope dying and fear rampant, Lim's older brother (who had been reunited with the family) was sent through the jungle to Thailand with his mother's wedding ring and some silver to buy food, but these few possessions were lost. The responsibility was then passed to Lim to barter some silver coins with Thai villagers for food that he could take back across the border. He accompanied a small group of people into the jungle, all of them knowing they could be shot by the Khmer Rouge or the Vietnamese, or maimed or even killed by land mines.

"I saw a lot of people killed in the jungle by booby traps," Lim recalled. "One experience in particular has left me with a very bad gag reflex. (I'm a dentist's nightmare!) I was flat on my stomach getting a drink of water from a foxhole. The water tasted slimy and oily. I spat it out, looked up, and saw a dead boy floating in the water just a few feet away. Even now I get nauseous thinking about it! I also got malaria during this trip and was left in the jungle for three days by myself until my fever broke, and then I went back by myself."

Lim made a few more jungle excursions back and forth between Thailand and Cambodia. He took his mother to a refugee camp in Thailand and went back for his brothers. But before he could lead his brothers out, his mother returned with a report that a huge battle was raging around the refugee camp involving the Khmer Rouge, the

Vietnamese, and the Thais. Fearing that their sons would be drafted into the Vietnamese army, the whole family made what was to be the final trip to Thailand. There, Lim's mother placed him and his younger brother in a refugee orphanage while she and her other two sons stayed in another refugee camp. By splitting up, they hoped chances would be better in finding someone who would sponsor a move to the United States.

Their prayers were answered in 1981.

Lim's mother put in an application through the U.S. Embassy in Thailand, and was eventually sponsored by the Catholic Social Ministry for relocation to America. Reunited when sponsorship was definite, Lim and his family came to the United States on November 11, 1981.

Lim said, "We came to Oklahoma because that was where our sponsor was. We didn't know where we would end up, but anywhere would have been fine."

The family was free at last.

Lim, sixteen years old at the time, worked like a demon to fit into the country that had adopted him. Taking five English classes a week to learn the language, he also resumed his long-neglected education.

"In Cambodia, I went to school only through the first grade," Lim said. "I flunked the test that would have allowed me into the next grade, but as things turned out it wouldn't have made a difference anyway. It was probably for the best that I didn't have an education!"

In Oklahoma, Lim was placed in the eighth grade because of his age. In the fall of 1982, he enrolled at Northeast High School and later transferred to John Marshall High School, graduating with honors in 1986 at the "ripe old age" of twenty-one. That fall, he entered Oklahoma City University to study premed.

During his first year of college, Lim attended a Cambodian Christian conference in Bolivar, Missouri, where he met his wife-to-be, Sunn (Rachel) Chhunn.

"Rachel was the first girl I ever dated," Lim said. "I had converted from Buddhism to Christianity almost immediately upon arriving in Oklahoma, and started to get very active in the Christian faith. When I met Rachel, I discovered she had similar experiences in Cambodia. So our spiritual and cultural bonds were formed immediately. In fact, I changed over to dentistry as a career choice because I believed that in medicine I would lose a great deal of quality time with her. In the Asian culture, family is extremely important in one's life. For me, there is nothing more precious than my family. Since I was determined to stay in a health-related field, I chose dentistry. I've never regretted it."

Lim and Rachel were married in July 1990, just before Lim started dental school at Oklahoma University College of Dentistry— OUCOD. Their daughter, Mollina, was born in December 1992. A former elementary school teacher, Rachel began to devote her time exclusively to her family while Lim was completing his dental studies.

After enduring the horrors of their country's war, Lim's mother and brothers also found peace, happiness, and a measure of prosperity in their new country. Lim's older brother, Cheang, graduated from college and went to work for the Department of Public Safety in Seattle, Washington, as a special liaison for Asian minorities. His younger brother, Meng, became a student at Oklahoma City Community College preparing for a career in pharmacology. And baby brother Thong began to follow in Lim's initial footsteps and is a premed student at the University of Central Oklahoma.

"My mother is doing well, too," Lim said with pride. "She lives here in Oklahoma City and works as a housekeeper for a local surgeon." Following graduation from OUCOD, Lim entered a one-year general practice residency at Hennepin County Hospital in Minneapolis, Minnesota. He then opened a general dental practice in Owasso, Oklahoma.

A humble and deferential young man, Lim nevertheless beams with pride at what he considers one of his proudest achievements.

"When I converted to the Baptist [Christian] faith, I narrated the Bible in the Cambodian language onto cassette. It took me two years to do it. That was four years ago and, since then, the cassettes have been distributed worldwide by Hosanna, a non-profit religious organization. While I get some royalties from it, the real pleasure comes from reaching out to others from my country that otherwise would not have access to God's Word.

"My religion [relationship with God], like my family, is a source of strength for me. Every Wednesday and Sunday when I go to church, I thank God for the peace He has put in my heart, the strength He gave me to survive the ordeals my family endured, and for the deep appreciation I now have for life itself."

Heng Ly Lim would be the first Cambodian to graduate from OUCOD, and most likely is one of the very few, if not the only one, from his country to be educated in a U.S. dental school.

"Given my family's history as refugees," Lim said, "I am very attuned to issues of discrimination. I wondered if the biases my family endured in China and then in Cambodia would follow us to America. I am so happy to say that I've never felt that stigma throughout my time in Oklahoma or at the College of Dentistry. The faculty, staff, and my classmates at school have been wonderfully supportive."

Asked how he could sum up his many experiences, Lim paused only briefly and then said, "You know, many people take things for granted. But it's understandable, because they haven't faced the prospect of losing what they have. I didn't make it through the 1970s on my own. I had my family, I had the will to live (which got sorely tested), and I had God. With those three, you can't lose. Anything is possible if you put your mind to it, work hard at it, and ask for God's help. And if you really want to appreciate life, to see what depths we can descend in our inhumanity to others, and to what heights we can rise with faith and perseverance, go see *The Killing Fields*."

Chapter 4

Graduation

As a refugee boy living in Thailand, I could never have dreamed that one day I would be blessed enough to come to America, much less graduate with a doctorate degree. This was beyond my thinking ability. I truly believe that God has blessed me more than I have ever imagined or asked Him for. I remember how excited I was about graduating from dental school.

The big day was coming, but I didn't know what I was going to do to celebrate. I knew Rachel had planned to do something very special, but I didn't really know what it was. She was keeping everything a secret from me. She wanted it to be a big surprise. She had been working hard, saving for this party. Night and day she worked painting angel figurines for a meager salary, a couple of dollars an hour. I saw her talking to a few people at our church about my graduation party, but I pretended not to hear or know anything about it. This graduation accomplishment meant as much to her as it did to me. Without her support, I wouldn't have been able to finish dental school. I tried to stay out of her way by doing my own thing. I had one last requirement to fulfill at school before I could officially graduate.

I was alone in the locker room, cleaning out my belongings, deep in thought, thinking about how fast the time went by. It seemed like just yesterday when, on my first day of school, one of the professors walked in without a smile and, as serious as he could be, said, "Welcome to dental school. Look to your right and look to your left.

One of you will not be here next year."

Fifty-one other classmates were sitting in the lecture hall with me, and together we were shocked by what this professor had just said. I looked to my left and my right as instructed. And I thought that this professor was either trying to scare me, or he was trying to tell me something very important. I looked at his face and tried to squeeze out every drop of truth from his words. I tried to make lemonade when he threw me a lemon. And what I gathered from his face was that dental school was going to be very hard, and that I would have to persevere to succeed.

I have to be honest with you—I was intimidated by what the professor said. However, I was more than determined to face the challenge of dental school. Nothing was going to stop me. I remember thinking that if I could survive the Khmer Rouge's regime for four years, I could make it through this. With God on my side, I could definitely do this.

The professor was right. The dental student who was sitting to my right didn't make it through the first year. The delicate balancing act between family and the highly strenuous demand of school work was excessively stressful for him. He developed a severe bleeding ulcer and had to be hospitalized.

Dental school was extraordinarily difficult, and could be overwhelming at times. Someone had put a picture up on the bulletin board in one of the clinics to inspire us students not to give up. It was a picture of a frog being swallowed by a crane. The frog's head was in the mouth of the bird, but the bottom half of the frog was dangling outside the bird's beak. At a glance, it looked like this frog was in a pickle. But when one examined the picture closely, one could see there was still hope for the struggling frog. It had its right hand choking the crane's neck. Below the picture was a caption that read, "Never give up!"

At the time, I felt that I was in over my head, just like that frog. But I also felt like the crane had bitten off a little more than it could chew. And I knew for a fact there were a lot of students who felt the same way as I did. A few of my classmates got divorced. One class-mate who had a bleeding ulcer had to drop out of school for a year.

School got much more difficult during my junior year. Mollina, our first daughter, was born. She brought us much joy and much pain. To know that our child was born in a free country that can offer her so much opportunity brought us immense joy. But, Mollina was a colicky baby. She cried all the time during her first three months of life, causing us to stay up most nights. We took turns staying awake to take care of her. Many times we drove her around in the night to calm her. It was a very difficult time, trying to study for dental school without sleep.

At night, Rachel tried to paint her miniature angels. Most of the time, we were struggling financially, but no one knew it. We took a lot of student loans to subsidize our needs. In the summer, I worked in the medical school as a research assistant. But we never complained. And Rachel always made sure I got a home-cooked meal. In my lunch box for school, she would put a china dish, a glass, a fork and spoon, a cloth napkin, and food. It might be only a chicken neck and rice, but it was first-class. I was the envy of my classmates. Sometimes we ran out of food, and I had to go catch fish from the lake. We even tried to eat shad and minnows, not know-ing that they were fish bait. I knew we didn't have any money for food when my wife handed me the fishing pole and said, "Let's go fishing!"

Before I knew it, four years had gone. It didn't seem like it was that long ago when I had come in as a freshman and the school assigned me these three lockers. I had learned and grown a lot. I was grateful for the opportunity, and for all the investments various men and women had poured into my life in the last four years. During this time, there were countless hours of lessons, lectures, homework, final tests, the national board exam, the state board exam, and all the sleep-less nights. Now it was over. I was there to clean out my lockers and to get them ready for an upcoming freshman. I thought about how proud my father would have been if he had only known that his son would graduate to become the first doctor ever in our family.

I was crying and praising God for His providential guidance and protection for my life. I must have stayed there for a long time, because eventually a janitor came in and asked me if I was all right. I wiped my tears and told him I was okay. I took my things out of my locker and put them in a cardboard box. I had accumulated a lot of stuff—books, dental instruments, stone models of teeth, school notes, and many pictures of my wife and daughter. I tossed the stone models and some of my old notebooks in the trash.

I checked one more time to make sure I didn't leave anything valuable behind. And then, with my box in my hands, I walked out of the building into the parking lot. When I got outside to the car, I turned back to look at my school for the last time, and I cried again. I had no idea where that emotion came from. It was like a floodgate had opened, and I couldn't stop it. It wasn't tears of sadness, but tears of joy mixed with gratefulness. I couldn't believe that I was actually graduating as a dentist. Who would believe that an illiterate sixteen-year-old boy from the jungles of Cambodia could finish college and graduate as a dentist in twelve years?

My friends didn't. When we were in high school struggling to learn English, CJ and Sam, my Cambodian friends, told me to quit school and get a job. They said that school was too hard and we were too old to learn a new culture and language.

"Many people are born here and they don't make it through high school. What makes you think that you can, especially to become a doctor?" Sam questioned me.

CJ quoted an old Cambodian saying to remind me, "Heng, short arms can't embrace the mountain."

"My goal is high, but it is not impossible," I reasoned with them. "It's a matter of how badly I want it, and how much I am willing to put forth the effort."

"Heng, you have great ambition, but for me, I am just trying to survive," Sam replied.

My friends and I knew that the pathway to higher education was going to be very difficult, and none of us were sure if we were going to accomplish it without help. At that time, I had just started learning about my new faith in God. I shared with them a scripture that I had just learned and memorized. The scripture told us to trust God with all our hearts and not to depend on our own understanding, but in all our ways to acknowledge Him, and He would lead our paths.

Sam shook his head, protesting that he didn't believe in God. He asked an incredibly difficult question, "If God is so good, how come He allowed so many good people to suffer and die?"

I told him that I didn't have all the answers, but that the new faith I had found in Christ had given me so much peace and confidence with life that I felt like a new person.

Both of my friends were orphans. Their parents were killed by the communists. They carried so much heartache and so many scars with them. It was probable that they had overwhelming post-traumatic stress disorder. At night, all of us had nightmares. Their minds were still occupied with trying to bury the past. And I could understand where they were coming from. I, too, had great difficulty focusing on school and work, but I had to let go of my past.

One of my teachers gave me wonderful advice. He said, "Yesterday is history. Tomorrow is a mystery. But today is a gift from God, and that is why we call it the present."

CJ informed me he was going to quit school and move out of state where many refugees were on welfare and they didn't have to work. I argued that we should be thankful for the government assistance, but that we should depend on it for only a short time.

"The price of getting something for nothing could cost us everything," I said, quoting what Father Joseph—a Catholic priest who sponsored our family to come to America—said regarding welfare. The priest said that the welfare system was a wonderful benevolence for those who were in dire need, but not for those could work or go to school.

Sam agreed with me. He said that he was going to do his best not to drop out of school. He was determined to make the most of his life and not to be like some young refugees who wasted their lives by joining groups of gangs, going around robbing people, and doing drugs. Sam called these people "crocodiles."

"Do you remember the story of the Old Man and the Crocodile?" Sam asked CJ and me. "That was one of the stories we heard while we were in the orphanage in Thailand," Sam added.

"Vaguely," CJ responded, wondering where he was going with this.

"There is a lesson we can learn from this," Sam explained to us, and then proceeded to tell the story.

There was once an old man traveling alone on a very hot summer day in a desert. He rode on a rustic wooden wagon pulled by a yoke of oxen. Suddenly, he came upon the most unusual scene—a stranded crocodile. The old man stopped to see if the beast was still alive. "Please, old man, take me to the water," the helpless and desiccated beast begged.

The old man had compassion for the poor crocodile, but he was too old and too weak. "Crocodile, I really want to help you, but I am not strong enough to carry you to the water," the old man sadly responded.

Again, the crocodile begged the old man, "Please do something, anything, but don't let me die here, sir."

The old man thought hard and long until, suddenly, his face lit up with a smile. "Crocodile, if I can tie you up with a rope, I can drag you behind my wagon to the water."

The painful thought of being tied with a braided rope, and getting dragged behind a yoke of oxen in rough terrain scared the crocodile, but he was desperate. The beast reluctantly agreed to the old man's idea.

With the crocodile tied and being dragged behind his wagon, the old man was now on a search for water. He searched long and hard, but finally he found a small lake.

Arriving severely scuffed and torn, the crocodile was still alive, "Please, old man, put me in the water, I have no strength to walk," the beast gently pleaded. The kind old man did as requested, dragging him into the water until he was ankle deep. The large beast soaked his sponge-dry body in the cool, refreshing water and he could feel that he was slowly regaining his strength. "Take me deeper into the water!" it demanded. So the old man did as he was told.

Not satisfied at waist deep water, the ungrateful crocodile showed his long teeth, commanding the old man to take him deeper into the water. Fearful for his life, the timid old man hesitated, but the crocodile vigorously insisted with slaps of his tail. The old man took the beast into the deep.

Now the crocodile sneered at the old man, "Old man, back there when I was helpless, you tied me up too tight and you dragged me too fast and rough. You caused me much unnecessary suffering. When you dragged me into the water, you didn't take me into the deep until I begged you." And with that said, the ungrateful beast opened up his big mouth to devour the kind old man.

"The story had a very sad ending, but it has a good teaching lesson," Sam said to CJ and me. And this was his point: that each one of us was a desperate and hopeless refugee stuck in a camp without a future or a country to call our home. Our sponsors were kind enough to bring us here to America. Therefore we must do our best to show our gratitude.

My friends and family have always been grateful for our new opportunity in America, especially our educational opportunity. CJ and Sam told me that they would love to continue going to school if at all possible. Unfortunately they lacked support from their family, and shortly after we had our serious talk, they both quit school. Both of them worked in a restaurant as dishwashers. Sam moved to California, where he died from liver disease shortly after dropping out of high school. I was deeply saddened at his death. CJ, my other friend, moved to another state.

In contrast with CJ and Sam, I had another friend who was full of determination and persevered to make the most of his life, even though he had a really difficult past as well as physical hardship.

Sothear came to America at the same time as CJ, Sam, and I did. From his external appearance, Sothear looked like he had the least potential of all of us. He was born with both club hands and club feet. As a little boy growing up in Cambodia during the Khmer Rouge's regime, Sothear was starved and sick to the point of losing his eyesight. His mother told me that Sothear only recovered part of his sight, and that he was still considered legally blind.

Sothear started to learn how to read and write English when he came to America as a teenager. To help him see letters on a page, he used a magnifying glass that looked more like a binocular lens. To make the situation even worse, Sothear's family was very poor. His mother was a widow making minimum wage with five little children. His outlook appeared to be dim and hopeless.

But Sothear had something extraordinary within him. He had the spirit of perseverance. As a young man, Sothear put his faith and trust in God, and he had the passion to make a difference with his life and with those around him.

When we were teenagers, Sothear and I used to go to church together. We were in the same Sunday school class. Our teacher, Norman Cantrell, would not accept any excuse for our failures. He often reminded us that, "Excuses are lies wrapped with reasons."

Norman insisted that we read and memorize the Scripture. He suggested that we should read one chapter of the Book of Proverbs each day. "This is vitamins for your soul," Norman told us. He asked us to underline the verse, "Trust in the LORD with all thine heart; and lean not unto thine own understanding. In all thy ways acknowledge him, and he shall direct thy paths" (Proverbs 3:5–6).

Sothear persevered through high school. He went to a school for the blind in Muskogee, Oklahoma. No one thought that he was going to be able to learn how to read and write. No one thought that he was going to be successful in life . . . no one except Sothear. Even his mother had doubts, but she faithfully prayed for him. His peers made fun of him, and many called him all kind of names. But he persevered. Sothear graduated from high school. Then he attended college, majoring in physical education.

His perseverance paid off when he graduated from college. And immediately after his graduation, he volunteered to serve with the Peace Corps in Jamaica. Now Sothear is living with his wife and three daughters in Maryland, where he is working as a teacher. He is living the American dream. From the beginning, Sothear's life didn't appear very promising, but with his spirit of determination and his trust in God, Sothear was able to accomplish what others could only dream of. He didn't seem to have as much talent as his peers did, but he had a great attitude. With his mother's prayers and his attitude of perseverance, Sothear demonstrated one of the most important truths that often gets overlooked—perseverance is better than talent, and attitude is better than ability.

There are many people who may have everything going for them. They may have all the opportunity, talent, ability, and even resources, but without the spirit of perseverance and determination, they won't go very far in life. Some people cower when they face adversity instead of persevering. They don't realize that God is only one prayer away.

My wife bought a beautiful picture frame that illustrates this truth. It says that when life is too hard to stand . . . kneel. Humbling ourselves on our knees, praying to God, is telling Him that we are weak and in desperate need of His help. God loves the meek, and He resists the proud. When we are weak, that is when He is strong.

I don't think I faced as much adversity as my friend Sothear did, but my wife and I had our share of trials, especially when I was going to dental school. We were on our knees a lot, praying. There were many occasions that we were without sleep and studying for final tests. Rachel was always up with me, making coffee and snacks for us as my classmates and I studied through the night. As a couple, we went through a lot together. But now, four years of dental school had gone by, and I was ready to graduate. I couldn't wait for my "surprise" party.

Rachel fervently worked to put a big graduation party together. She cooked egg rolls and stir-fried rice and vegetables. She invited our entire church family and the whole Cambodian community to help us celebrate. My family, along with Rachel's, came. They were very proud of my achievement. With the hard-earned money from her angel painting, Rachel bought me a very extravagant graduation gift—a Gucci watch, a gift to treasure for a lifetime.

Chapter 5

Our Attitude Determines Our Altitude

In the next few chapters, I am going to take time to share with you what I believe is one of the most important secrets to life. Our life on earth is a journey. It begins at conception and it ends as the last breath fades from our body. Everything we do, and everything we don't do, between these two events is molded by our thinking and attitude.

Many people just exist. Day in and day out, they just go through the motions, telling themselves they are victims. They are conditioned to believe that they can't be better. They embrace the "poor me" mentality and become weighted down by it all. In India, people live in the caste into which they are born, and most of them believe there is nothing anyone can do to change their fate. No matter what situation people are born into, God can bring positive change. No matter how destructive the circumstances, God can bring about something better. All we need to understand is this one simple truth: God wants a better life for us. He loves us and wants us to live life to the fullest. God loves and cares for us, and He gives us the ability that He gave to no other creature on earth. He gives us the ability to control our own minds and attitudes.

Abraham Lincoln, the sixteenth president of the United States, said, "A man is as happy as he makes up his mind to be."

Viktor Frankl, a survivor of the Nazi concentration camps, said, "We who lived in the concentration camps can remember the men who walked through the huts comforting others, giving away their last piece of bread. They may have been few in number, but they offer sufficient proof that everything can be taken from a man but one thing: the last of the human freedoms—to choose one's attitude in any given set of circumstances, to choose one's own way."

Just like we can work our body and build our muscles, so can we work our thoughts and build our attitude. Consider the best musician you can think of. To become that good, the musician had to practice over and over until each note was perfected. I can promise you that without practice, that musician could not improve. That's how it is with our attitude. If we don't practice having a good attitude, we will not get better.

Like Viktor Frankl, I, too, as a survivor of the Cambodian Killing Fields, also witnessed what Dr. Frankl spoke of regarding the concentration camps. Even in the most desperate circumstances of life, people still have the freedom to choose their own attitude.

When I was in the first grade, a teacher made me memorize a few lines, and those words formed the way I believed. He said:

I have a dream that one day I will have a little house by the mountain, built by the river, with a beautiful, large tree to give shade. Surrounding the house, I will have a garden where I will grow all kinds of herbs, vegetables, and flowers. This garden will produce food and provide enjoyment. I will raise horses, cows, chickens, and ducks. I will raise these animals, and then I will take them to the market to make money.

Cambodia was a terrifying place for a child. I was the second oldest of six children. I had just begun to understand fear. When I was seven years old, my father was abducted by a guerilla warfare group—the Khmer Rouge. Even in a war-torn country like Cambodia, my father would laugh, still trying to keep some semblance of sanity. But, suddenly, he was gone. That's when I truly knew what fear was. The leader of our home had been snatched away from his family by a group of men who took what they wanted, and they didn't care who or what got in their way, or who was hurt in the process.

My mother found herself alone with six children, the oldest being ten and the youngest just a few days old. It wasn't until I was an adult that I was able to fully understand what my mother must have felt. She must have been terrified, but she never let us see it. She knew that if her children saw the full extent of her fear they would have never been able to make it through the whole ordeal. My mother became our rock!

We lived in a shack no bigger than a one-car garage. We had no running water. To get water, we had to carry the water from the river which ran through the area. There was no electricity, so when the sun went down, there was only darkness. In the corner of the house were charred stones which we used to cook what little food we could find, but at least they were our stones. We really couldn't cook on the rocks, but we warmed up food on them to make it a little more tolerable.

Conditions were terrible. No human should ever have to live like that. It was filthy, and we had no medical care. Two of my siblings died because of the horrid living conditions. We were starving. There was so little food, and any food we could find had to be split between all of us. I remember trying to be strong and not cry, but at times I couldn't help it.

I had to leave school. The one place that I could depend on for learning new things, and that had put wonderful words in my memory, had been stripped from me. I couldn't stay in school because I had to help take care of my family. For the next eight years we lived on almost nothing. It was a time of darkness, a defining time for millions of Cambodians. Those years defined who we were as a people. We had every right to be bitter. Everything we knew and everything we owned had been taken from us. They had left us broken. Our beliefs and attitudes were molded during this time.

We were victims. I remember when our father was returned to us he was a different man. I watched the life leave his body as he took his last breath in my mother's arms.

When I was fourteen, my family escaped the Killing Fields of Cambodia, and two years later we found our way to the United States of America, where I ended up in Oklahoma City. I spoke no English and had the education of a first grader. If anyone deserved to have a terrible attitude, it was me. As a child, I had seen more death and destruction than many soldiers. I had been in places that would make other people pass out from fright. I had eaten things that would make others sick, but I had to do it to survive.

I had a choice. I could let my life be defined by what had happened to me up to this point, or I could define my life by what I knew I could accomplish. I chose the latter. In the next several years, I studied and learned. I learned the language, the culture, and a new faith. I had some of the best teachers and mentors, including my mother, my Sunday school teachers, my high school and college teachers, my pastors, Dr. Anthony Jordan and Dr. Jack Thompson, my sponsors, Dr. and Mrs. Peter Denman and Mr. and Mrs. John Harrington. Most of all, I learned who I was and what the word "potential" really meant.

For twelve years I applied myself and never gave up. After those twelve years, I stepped away from the University of Oklahoma commencement ceremony as Dr. Heng Ly Lim. I was awarded the Asian-American Outstanding Professional Multicultural Achievement Award 1993–94. I was one of five hundred other doctors that applied to do my residency in one of the most prestigious hospitals in the world. Out of five hundred applicants, only four would be chosen. I was one of the four. It seems like a lifetime ago that I read that acceptance letter. I can still remember the lump in my throat as I saw the word "Congratulations" in that letter.

Today, I am happily married, with a beautiful wife of more than twenty years. Rachel and I have two daughters. I practice neuro-muscular and cosmetic dentistry in my own world-class dental facil-ity in Owasso, Oklahoma. My office was the first dental office in Oklahoma to have a GENDEX 3-D (CT scan) scanner. I live in my dream home, just a few miles from Lake Oologah.

Am I telling you this so you will know how fantastic I think I am? No, I'm telling you this so you can realize that if Heng Lim can do this, so can you. I'm telling you this so that you too will under-stand that your attitude can determine your future. You may have all the talent, charm, looks, and resources in the world. However, if you don't have a good attitude, these things will not take you very far in life. Talent is a gift from God—if you don't use it, it will be a waste.

Benjamin Franklin said, "Hide not your talents, they for use were made, What's a sundial in the shade?"

There have been many talented people who have failed to accom-plish much in life, simply because they never started. Others have failed simply because they gave up too early. Thomas Edison said, "Many of life's failures are people who did not realize how close they were to success when they gave up."

The secret to success is to know what you want to do. Have a goal. This way you will know what to ask God to help you with. God is there to help, but you have to ask Him to guide you and bless you. You control what your attitude looks like.

I knew when I was a young boy in war-torn Cambodia that I wanted to help people. Deep inside of me, there was a doctor that needed to get out. I believed that one day I would be able to improve people's lives medically; I knew it beyond a shadow of doubt. That is why twelve years after I stepped foot in this country, I graduated as a doctor.

Did I know when I was ten how I was going to accomplish this? Of course not! Did I know when I was sixteen how I would learn to speak English? Heavens, no! Did I know when I was sixteen that I would become a doctor? You bet I did! I knew it, because it was my goal and my passion. Too many people today live their lives never even trying to find their passion, and that makes me very sad. Many people want results, but they are not willing to put the effort into it. They are too lazy!

Even if you don't know what it is you are passionate about right now, it is important that you understand that you need to be looking for something. If we are always searching, then our approach will be much more open to things we may never have thought possible. Looking for your passion will also protect you from the dangers of falling back into the past. If you are always facing forward, looking for what it is that you want, you won't fall back so quickly into the trap of feeling sorry for yourself when things don't go the way you expect them to go. It's important to remember that failure can have either a positive or negative influence on your success.

If you look at those whom you would consider to be unsuccessful, my guess is that those individuals don't take responsibility for their own failures. They are quick to place the blame on someone else. They look for any reason they can find to point a finger in any direction other than at themselves. Until they stop blaming their failures on someone else, and start taking the responsibility for their own situations, they will never succeed. Taking responsibility is up to each of us. Let's stop coming up with excuses. The next time you fail at something, instead of immediately thinking of excuses, look into the mirror and simply tell yourself that you must not have wanted it bad enough.

Another man made the journey to the United States at the same time my family did. His name was also Heng. We both arrived in Oklahoma City at the same time. We both knew nothing of the language; we were both scared; and we both had been through the same kinds of things in Cambodia. The adversity we faced was the same, but he chose to deal with it differently. He committed suicide by hanging himself. I have often wondered what was so different between the two of us, and I finally realized that the only difference was that I had a different attitude toward life. Because of my trust in God, and because I had taken responsibility for my actions, I handled adversity differently than he did.

How we handle adversity determines our character. When you face adversity, you have two options. One is to retreat and become a victim; the other is to determine, without panic, how to overcome. You can become the victim or the victor, but you can't become the victor without going into the battle. Adversity is a universal test. It defines who you are and how you will proceed. When you fight adversity, your reward can be great. The problem is that many people, when faced with adversity, cower away from it. They don't understand that they can win if they will stand up to it and fight. Even nature teaches us that: salmon have to fight upstream to thrive. The dead ones float downstream.

History also tells us of many people that have become champions over adversity. People like Joseph, the son of Jacob, who was sold into slavery but later emerged as prime minister of Egypt. People like Ruth, the Moabite, who lost her husband to death, but later married Boaz and became the grandmother of the second king of Israel.

Here is a story that I am sure we have all heard, but it fits so well with the subject of how attitude can help to overcome adversity that I just have to share it again. Centuries ago the Philistines went to war against the Hebrew people. The Philistines were great in number and power. They wanted to make the people of Israel their slaves. The Philistines and Israelites met in Judah at a place called Oak Valley. Both groups were ready for battle. The Philistines were on one hill and the Israelites were on the opposite hill, with only a valley separating the two armies. From the Philistine camp, a giant who was nearly ten feet tall stepped out from the ranks and made his way into the open field. He was wearing a bronze helmet that covered his head and reflected the power of the sun. His body was covered by armor that had battle scars all over it. He carried a bronze sword and a spear that was the size of a small tree. In front of him, a shield carrier led the way. The sight alone of the warrior was enough to send a chill of fear down the spine of every Israelite that was a witness to the killer dressed as a soldier.

With a voice that matched his stature, the giant called to the Israelites, "Why bother your whole army? Am I not Philistine enough for you? You are all committed to your King Saul aren't you, so pick the best fighter among you and send him here to fight me. If your soldier kills me, on my word, every Philistine will be your slave, but if I kill your best, then all Israelites will be slaves to the Philistines. I challenge the troops of Israel this day. Give me a man, and let us fight together."

When King Saul and all of the Israelites heard this challenge, they were terrified and lost all hope. How were they going to defeat this giant called Goliath? We need to understand from this part of the story that adversity can paralyze us with fear. It is important as we go into adversity's battles that we remain clear-minded and understand that fear is our enemy, just like Goliath.

At this same time, there was a young boy named David, who was the son of Jesse. Three of David's seven brothers had joined forces with Saul and were on the hill as the great Goliath proclaimed his challenge. While David's brothers were out on the battlefield preparing for war with the Philistines, David remained at home and tended the family sheep. David was a good shepherd, doing everything in his power to protect and defend the sheep in his care.

For forty days, the Philistines and the Israelites were on those hills in Oak Valley, and every morning and evening Goliath would make his challenge, waiting for just one soldier to take him at his word, but that soldier never came.

One morning Jesse told his son David to take some supplies to his brothers and King Saul while they were in Oak Valley. He wanted David to get a report on how things were going and how his brothers were. Jesse was concerned and he missed his sons. The next morning

David was up before dawn, preparing for his trip. With his supplies ready, David made his way to Oak Valley. David left the food he brought with a sentry and ran to the troops where he found his brothers. Goliath came out and once again offered his challenge, but this time something was different. This time David heard his words. David couldn't believe his eyes. The Israelites cowered away from this giant. They retreated as fast as they could. David heard the soldiers talking about the situation. They had never seen anything like this. None knew of a man that would take the challenge and stand up to Goliath, but everyone knew that if there were such a man among them, and that if that man did kill Goliath, then his reward would be great. He would live the rest of his days in want for nothing. They also knew that no man among them would do it.

David couldn't believe what he was hearing. He asked some soldiers standing around him, "What is the reward for the man who kills this Philistine? Who will take and wipe this stain from the fabric of our nation? Who does this filthy grossness of a man think he is, anyway, daring to try and intimidate God's people?" The soldiers told David what the king had said about the reward for the man who killed the giant. Later that day, one of David's brothers found him and asked him what he was doing there. Why wasn't he tending the sheep? David responded that he was asking about what had happened. He didn't understand why not one Israelite would stand up to this bully. No one had the right to challenge God's people like that. David told his brother that Goliath was just a man; that he was not stronger than God; and that God would take care of any one of His people that would stand and fight.

Someone who overheard David's conversation with his brother went to King Saul and told him what had been said. When Saul heard of this boy talking so much like a man, he summoned the young David to come to his tent. David entered the king's tent and was asked his reason for making such statements. David's reply was, "Your Majesty, no one needs to fear this Philistine. I will fight him."

"You?" asked King Saul. "You are no more than a child. This giant will tear you limb from limb and eat your flesh. How could you possibly think you could win?"

"God is on our side, Majesty. I may be young, but I understand the strength of God. I have killed a lion and a bear while tending my flock, and now I know that those beasts were put in my path so that I could practice for this day. God is with me and He will protect me."

"Very well, my young warrior, you shall fight Goliath." Saul had his servants put the king's armor on David. He was covered with the beauty of Saul's protection and handed Saul's sword, but David couldn't move. It was all too heavy. It made David stagger and stumble. David told them that it was too much. He told them that he wasn't a soldier and that he didn't want to put on any of the gear a warrior would need. He told them there was only one weapon for him to use. It was a weapon he trusted—his slingshot.

The king was amazed at this young shepherd, but he was also very nervous for him. He watched as David went to a nearby stream, chose five smooth stones, and put them in his pouch. David checked his sling, reached in and caressed the smooth stones, and then went to find Goliath, the Philistine champion.

Goliath was easy to find. He had just stepped out again to give his challenge. When he was finished, he watched for the men to retreat as they had always done, but this time was different. This time he saw a figure coming toward him. Goliath couldn't believe it. This wasn't a man coming toward him; it was just a boy. This made Goliath angry, and he shouted at David: "Who are you to fight me? You are just a boy. And what is that stick in your hand? Do you think I am a dog? Get closer, and I will kill you and throw your dead body to the birds!"

David continued to walk toward the giant, and Goliath began to curse him. David said to Goliath, "You come with your sword and your spear. You have the strength of many men. But I have come with the Name of God on my lips! He is stronger than one hundred of you put together, and since you have cursed me, you have also cursed

Him. He will give me the victory, and today it will be you that the birds feed upon. God will give me the victory so that all will know that He is the one true God!"

David picked up speed and ran toward Goliath. As he ran, he reached into his pouch and grabbed one of the stones. He pulled it out and placed it in his sling. Goliath watched in amazement as this boy came running toward him. David, now in a full-out run, swung the sling 'round and 'round above his head. He could hear the sling's pouch cutting through the wind as he approached. In the blink of an eye, David let the sling go and the stone flew with great speed through the air. It happened so fast that Goliath had no time to react. The stone hit the giant right in the middle of the forehead.

David stopped and watched as Goliath stood there with a dazed look on his face. Goliath was stunned. His knees started to buckle under all of his weight and, like a tree, he fell backward to the ground. A great cloud of dust flew around him. David ran and picked up Goliath's sword, and as quickly as he had spun the rock, he plunged the sword into the giant's neck, killing him right there and cutting off his head. Goliath was dead, and the Philistines fled in terror.

What an amazing story! But it didn't end there. David would be used by God throughout his entire life and would one day become king over Israel. You see, Goliath represents the adversity in all our lives. If Goliath had not challenged the Israeli army, David would not have been able to overcome him. Just like the giant in the story, our adversity can be huge and terrifying, but it can also be defeated.

Chapter 6

Dare to Dream

History is a great teacher. If we will simply learn from its pages, we will find some extraordinary people who learned that life is difficult but didn't embrace excuses. Consider this: What if, a couple thousand years ago, a small boy had thought, "I am just a shepherd. I will never make anything of myself." If that had happened, we may not have known King David, the second king of Israel. What if, a hundred years ago, a young paper boy would have thought to himself, "I am nobody; I just throw papers." The bulb that lights our way may have never been invented by Thomas Edison. In 1968, if Bill Gates had said, "It's just tic-tac-toe on the computer and no one will want to do that," the only windows in houses across the world would be those that look out into the neighborhood.

All three of these men, and thousands of men and women like them, knew one thing: they knew how to avoid the "if only." When they looked into the mirror, they saw something magnificent. As you read through this book, if you will apply the principles printed on its pages, I promise that you too will be able to look into the mirror and see something truly extraordinary.

Every so often I have to look into the mirror to see my inner self. The last time I looked into the mirror, something really great happened. I got better looking! I saw the way God sees me for who I am in Christ instead of the way I usually see myself as an ordinary man.

Finding the extraordinary person in the mirror will be a journey, and every journey starts somewhere. There is an old proverb that says, "A journey of a thousand miles begins with the first step." It sounds simple to just take that first step, but how can we take that first step if we don't know what it is? I can help you with that. The first step is belief. You see, your belief is your reality.

Here is what Brian Tracy says in his bestselling book *Maximum Achievement.* "Perhaps the biggest mental roadblocks that you will ever have to overcome are those contained in your self-limited beliefs. . . . They hold you back by stopping you from ever trying. They often cause you to see things that are simply not there." Excuses and the "if onlys" are exactly what Brian is talking about.

Let me acquaint with you a story about beliefs, using one of the most massive of God's creations, the elephant. A few years ago I took my family to see an ancient stone temple in Cambodia called Angkor Wat. This temple was built in the twelfth century (nine hundred years ago) by a king named Suryavarman II. There is a moat that surrounds the entire temple that is 625 feet wide. There is also a wall around the complex that has a total length of two and a quarter miles. Inside that wall and moat are hundreds and hundreds of acres of beautiful land where the temple stands. Over five million tons of sandstone was used to build this temple. It took thousands of workers and over one hundred years to complete this Cambodian masterpiece.

As my family and I stood there, letting our imaginations run away with thoughts of ancient life, one of the questions as to how this place was built was answered when two incredibly beautiful elephants walked by us. When the temple was built, elephants were used to move the sandstone blocks into place. Hundreds of these creatures were used to provide the strength to move the blocks of stone needed to build this structure.

Today these bigger-than-life animals are used for moving an entirely different material for the temple. They are used to give rides to tourists. As I watched these creatures amble past, it made me understand the word "belief" a little bit better. Here was a creature that weighed several tons, but with the poke of a stick, it did exactly what it believed it had been trained to do. It made me also think of circus elephants. In a circus, the elephant will do stunning tricks. Their trainer or master will utter a word, and open his arms like a symphony conductor, and the elephant will stand on one leg with its trunk in the air. The audience is amazed at the trick and erupts with applause. Does the elephant do this trick because of the applause? No, it does the trick because for years its master has made it believe that standing on one leg in front of the audience is what it is supposed to do. The fact is that the elephant is a wild animal, but it has been trained to believe it is something different.

What do you believe? Do you believe that you can do anything you want? Or do you believe that you are doing elephant tricks and there is nothing you can do to change that? Our beliefs determine our actions.

Recently a friend and I were talking about events in American history, and he told me a story he had come across about a slave that had been freed because of the Civil War. The freed slave had acquired some land. One afternoon he was plowing his land, getting ready to plant his crops. As the sweat ran down his brow, he heard in the distance a voice that sent a chill down his spine. It was the voice of his former master. The former master was yelling at the freed man to get him a drink of water. The farmer turned and looked at this shell of a man that used to be his master.

The former master said, "Slave, did you hear me? Fetch me some water!" Like the elephant, the freed man had been programmed his entire life to believe that he was to always be in service to his master. On this day, he was standing behind his own plow, working his own land with his own mule. He realized that *he* was in control of his belief, and not his former master. It was because of this realization that he was able to look his peer in the eye and say, "Fetch your own water."

With those words of freedom, the farmer went back to work.

Henry Ford once said, "If you think you can, or you think you can't—you're right." Change the word *think* in Ford's quote to *believe,* and really try to understand the power in this word. This one seven-letter word can change your life. The power of that word can hold you back doing nothing but elephant tricks, or it can release you to follow your dreams.

I was born in Cambodia during one of the most turbulent times of its history. The country was torn apart by a revolutionary war. Times were dark and, for many, hopeless. But in the darkness of that chaotic time, there was a bright spot in my life. That bright spot was created by my first-grade teacher. I didn't know it then, but I know now that this teacher understood what the word "belief" meant. He had all of his students memorize the following:

> I have a dream that one day I will have a little house by the mountain, built by the river, with a beautiful, large tree to give shade. Surrounding the house, I will have a garden where I will grow all kinds of herbs, vegetables, and flowers. This garden will produce food and provide enjoyment. I will raise horses, cows, chickens, and ducks. I will raise these animals, and then I will take them to the market to make money.

It has been over forty years since my first-grade teacher taught me this. I will never forget the wonderful picture painted in my imagination when he described the house on the river and the garden that I would work in. It created such a wonderful picture in my mind that I didn't just memorize the words, but I said them over and over, thousands of times. I repeated it to myself when I was frightened or sad. I repeated it to myself when I was lonely or fighting for my life. It became the driving force that shaped me into who I am. It all comes down to this. What is your belief? What belief has taken you through thousands of nights?

I know there are those of you who, when you were young, may have had an adult influence in your life that used encouraging words that helped shaped your life. Right now you may be thinking that your words and mine are nothing alike. You may not have been told anything beautiful. You may have been told that you would never amount to anything. You may even have been told you that the world would be a better place if you just weren't in it, or that you were a mistake and you should have never been born. My heart breaks for you if you have been told these things. At times when you were afraid or when you were lonely, these words may have kept you company and, because of that, they became your belief. I have good news for you. You can change your belief.

"Life is pain. . . . Anyone who says differently is selling something." That is one of my favorite lines in the movie *The Princess Bride*. Life is hard, and because life can be so hard, we tend to hide from its difficulties. Do you remember as a child hearing the story of "The Grasshopper and the Ants"? It is a wonderful story that illustrates this idea. The grasshopper takes things easy, hiding from life's difficulties, but the ants do not. Sometimes we hide behind our beliefs, believing that life can never be what we imagine.

Do you want to know the secret to having a wonderful life? Change your beliefs. Doesn't that sound simple? Change your beliefs and that "if only" life we know and hide behind can be gone forever. Change your beliefs and let the person that you know is living inside of you come out.

If it is so simple to change our beliefs, then why don't more people do it? The reason is that we can't or, more probably, we don't know how to break the hold of our past. Our past is a powerful thing. It is our history, and it can be all we ever think about. Our past may be what we hide behind. We may use our past as our excuse not to change. Maybe we don't know how to function without holding onto our past. If that is how you feel, keep reading. You are just getting to the good part.

Our thoughts are automatically tied to our past. We don't even have to consciously think about it. Many of us spend our lives in the past. If someone were to ask us if we were trapped in the past, I am certain most of us would answer "no." But all it takes is a glimmer of a problem, and our past is where we choose to hide.

So what does all that mean? Change your thoughts and you will change your life. Have you ever heard the concept of "you reap what you sow"? It is a biblical principle that is taught throughout our entire life. The statement means that whatever you put time and effort into, that is what you will become. What have you become? My hope is that you will become who you want to be. Here are the stepping stones of the "reap what you sow" principle.

If you sow a thought, you reap an action.
If you sow an action, you reap a habit.
If you sow a habit, you reap a character.
If you sow a character, you reap a destiny.

Study after study has proven that what we think is what we will become. There is power in thought. Amazingly, scientists believe that we use only about two percent of the potential power of our brain. It is thought that even the smartest man in the world, Albert Einstein, only used ten percent of his brain. With something as powerful as the human brain, emotions like depression, anger, sadness, and jealousy can have a profoundly negative effect on how the brain works. Some people are bombarded with these emotions. They let themselves be programmed. If you are one of these people, here are some other emotions I want you to dwell on instead: happiness, joy, positivity, excitement. These emotions can generate great things. We have the power to think. We have the power to do complex things without really even thinking about it. We have the power to learn. We can learn how to change our thoughts from being negative to being positive. It is within each of us.

Here is a riddle for you. How does a Cambodian weed the garden? With a bulldozer! Several years ago, part of my ranch in Oklahoma was taken over by thorn trees, and it seemed that nothing I did got rid of them. They were like weeds in a garden. One day, I was talking to my neighbor about this problem, and a bulldozer found its way into our conversation. I asked my neighbor Bob if he knew how to drive a bulldozer, and he looked at me like I was crazy. It was like he was saying, "Of course I know how to drive a bulldozer; don't you?" He told me that he was an accomplished bulldozer operator and that if I would get one, he would be happy to bulldoze those pesky thorn trees down and they would never be an issue again.

After agreeing to the plan, I went into the house and made some phone calls. I rented the biggest and best bulldozer I could find, and it would be delivered on Saturday morning. I could hardly sleep on Friday as I thought of that huge piece of equipment coming to my house. I was as excited as a Cambodian goat roper at a Mexican rodeo—and that's excited!

The sun was barely up when my feet hit the floor. Today was the day! At about 6:15 a.m. I heard the sound of a large truck making its way up my driveway. I ran outside and there, sitting on that heavy-duty trailer, was a beautiful yellow bulldozer. Just behind the delivery truck was my friend Bob. He parked his truck and stood beside me as we waited for the man that delivered the machine to drive it off the trailer.

"You sure you know how to do this, Bob?"

"No problem, Heng. By the end of the day, all of these thorn trees will be a memory."

Bob and I listened as the bulldozer operator told us about all the gizmos and levers on the 'dozer. To Bob this was simple. It was like getting a lesson on driving someone else's car. For me, it was like listening to a foreign language. I didn't know anything that he was talking about, but there were a few things I picked up. I did listen carefully about how to make the 'dozer go forward and backward.

After a few minutes of the lesson, Bob put on his gloves, hopped into the driver's seat, and pushed the lever forward, causing the bulldozer to belch out a cloud of black smoke, and he started working on the project.

I was out there with Bob all day long, cutting trees with my chain-saw and watching Bob as he made that wonderful piece of equipment move across the dirt. It was as simple as a few pedals and a lever to make the blade go up and down. Not much to it at all. At about 6:30 p.m., Bob parked the bulldozer and we stood there together, admiring the work we had done. What had been thick and covered with thorny plants twelve hours earlier was now cleared off and ready for whatever new life I wanted to plant. It had been a good day. Bob stuck out his hand and I shook it, expressing to him how much I appreciated what he had done. With that, Bob got back into his truck and went home.

The next morning, I was up early again. I put on my boots and walked back out to where we had worked, and as I walked around the cleared piece of land, I noticed a big rock that I wanted to move. It was huge! I figured it had to weigh over thirty-five hundred pounds. How was I going to move that *huge* rock? Then it hit me. I had a bulldozer! I could move anything! It was a simple job. All I had to do was go forward twenty-five yards, turn to the left just a bit, put the blade down and push the rock about another fifteen feet. How hard could it be? Bob had done stuff a lot harder than that yesterday. I had watched what he did. I only had to go straight and make a little turn.

"I can do this," I said to myself.

So up onto the bulldozer's track I climbed. I was excited! My heart was pounding as I reached the cab. I looked in and there was the key just hanging there. *I can do this,* I thought. I opened the door and sat in the seat. It was intimidating. My body didn't even come close to filling the seat, but I still thought, *I can do this.* I reached down and turned the key. The motor sounded like the Berlioz Symphonie Fantastique as it came to life.

I couldn't contain my excitement. I heard myself say, "All right. This is cool!" I pushed the lever and I, too, made it belch black smoke. I pushed another lever with my foot, the 'dozer jerked forward, and I started going toward the rock. I looked out the windshield and realized I couldn't see the rock I wanted to move. I pushed another lever and the 'dozer made a hard left. It was going toward some mud, and just beyond that was a giant tree. My excitement turned to panic. I pushed further and the tractor started going faster. That was the wrong thing to do. I pulled all the way back on the lever and the machine stopped, but now the blade was caught on the tree and the tracks were in the mud. I tried to move the thing backward, but it wouldn't budge. I tried jiggling the 'dozer, but it just sank deeper and deeper into the mud.

Not knowing what else to do, I called Bob. He came over, shook his head, and kind of laughed. He had me get out of the seat. He got in, and in three minutes, the 'dozer was out and back in its place.

That day taught me a few very important things. One is that you can't jiggle a bulldozer. But more importantly, it taught me that you can have all the potential in the world, but if you don't learn how to use that potential, you can find yourself getting stuck. Could the bulldozer have moved the rock by itself? No, the bulldozer can do nothing on its own. Did the bulldozer have the potential to move that rock? Absolutely! It had the potential to do that, and much more. Was it possible for me to move that rock by myself? No, the rock was too big. Do I have the potential to drive that bulldozer? Yes, it is well within my ability to drive that bulldozer, I just had to learn how to do it. I had to learn how to unlock that potential within me to understand the mechanics of the bulldozer and how it works.

Have you ever thought about how much potential you have? We have a potential that is limited only by our imagination. Think of Ludwig Von Beethoven. When he wrote his fifth and most popular symphony, he knew he was going deaf. Here was a man that lived his entire life to create music, and he was losing the one sense that could make that creation come to life for him. Did that cause him to stop? No. Did it cause him to be frustrated? Absolutely, but he didn't allow that fear to turn into defeat. We learn to adapt. By the time Beethoven finished his ninth and final symphony, Beethoven was totally deaf. At the end of the ninth symphony's debut, the crowd erupted with a standing ovation. Beethoven was backstage and didn't even know the concert had finished. It wasn't until a young singer from the chorus took him by the arm and turned his attention to the audience that he was able to fully understand how much people loved his work.

Helen Keller is another great example of incredible potential. On June 27, 1880, Helen Keller was born a normal child. When she was nineteen months old, Helen contracted an illness that left her blind, deaf, and mute. Inspired by the writing of Charles Dickens, Helen's parents started a journey that would change the world. Through countless meetings, thousands of miles of travel, and introductions of people that would touch Helen's life, they found Anne Sullivan. Anne started working with Helen, but it seemed impossible that Helen would ever be able to understand.

Then one day, with water running over Helen's hand and with the determination of young Anne Sullivan, Helen understood. She understood that the movements in the palm of her hand meant W-A-T-E-R. Can you imagine the excitement in the lives of that student and teacher? Helen developed an insatiable appetite for learning. In 1904, Helen Keller was the first blind and deaf person to get a Bachelor of Arts degree. Helen wrote twelve books. She helped thousands and thousands of people, young and old alike, deal with their disabilities. Helen Keller was even awarded the highest civilian achievement of all, the Presidential Medal of Freedom.

I can hear you now: "Heng, hello? It's just me. I'm not like Beethoven or Helen Keller. I am just a simple person. They were great people that overcame something horrible. I can see and hear. I don't have those kinds of problems. My problem isn't physical. It's emotional."

I understand. I understand that what Beethoven and Helen Keller overcame may seem so much more difficult than what you might be going through, but the bottom line is this: the problems are the same. Physically or emotionally, if what you are going through causes you to be anything less than your very best, then it's time to change. All problems come down to the same two words: "I can't." The only thing different between you and these two great people in history is that they lived past their "I can't" time in life. They were not magical. They were part of the same group that you belong to. They were part of humanity, and because they were part of that extraordinary group, they learned how to say "I can."

It comes down to one thing—effort. Beethoven and Helen Keller both had to apply a tremendous amount of effort to what they did. As I write this, I can't even imagine what it was like for Helen Keller and Anne Sullivan to work together, day after day, without being able to understand what the other person was doing. They both put in the effort, and as a result, one day there was understanding. When Helen and Anne were out by the water pump, Helen's world suddenly made sense. Their effort was rewarded. With that one breakthrough, everything else in Helen's life was possible.

What kind of effort have you put into correcting your problem? What have you done to change your "I can't" to "I can"? Decide right now that you won't keep doing elephant tricks. Decide right now that you will make the effort to break the pattern of your thoughts and live outside your past. Decide that you want to be a different person. Decide that you can win!

Chapter 7

Moving to Oologah

During my last semester of dental school, I really didn't know where I was going to practice. One of my former Sunday school teachers, Dr. Bob Lee, graciously made me an offer.

"Heng, I will sell you my dental practice for a dollar."

I thanked him for his generosity, but told him I couldn't accept his offer. At the same time, one of my professors suggested that I should join the Navy. The idea of being a naval officer tempted me tremendously, so I contacted a recruiter. All the necessary arrangements were made, and I had made an appointment to meet with him to sign the official contract. But God had a different plan in mind for me. Consequently, the recruiter forgot the appointment; instead, he showed up the next day. That night I had changed my mind.

The following week, the assistant dean of the school, Dr. Kevin Avery, stopped me in the hall and asked me about the possibility of doing a general residency at a hospital in Minnesota. I came home and told Rachel about it. We prayed about it and decided that it was a good idea to move our family closer to her parents, who were living in Rochester, Minnesota. With Dr. Avery's help, we applied for the position.

There were between four and five hundred doctors applying for the same four positions, but I was blessed to be one of the doctors to be accepted. We thought that this was definitely God's plan for us.

Otherwise He would not have provided such an opportunity for us.

So, after graduating from dental school I had decided to move my family up to Minnesota. At the last minute, Rachel and I decided to tour the hospital one more time. While we were there, both of us realized we didn't feel any peace at all about this job, but neither of us was willing to admit this to the other. When we returned to Oklahoma City to get the rest of our things, we received a letter from Dr. Joe Maltsberger, a dentist from the Tulsa area. A few months earlier, he had read my story written by Dr. Frank Miranda, which had been printed in the University of Oklahoma Alumni Magazine.

Dr. Maltsberger felt compelled to extend to me an invitation to join his practice, and he asked me to come and visit Oologah, a little town which I thought sounded like it should be in Japan. Rachel and I came and surveyed it, and we fell in love with the area. We wanted to raise our family in a small-town atmosphere that offered conserva-tive family values and a great school system. Oologah had both. We accepted his offer and moved our family to this little town which had a population of 854.

Being the first Asian family in a very small town far away from all our family brought us much uncertainty at first. One of our fears was of not being accepted by the community. But the people in this community were very warm and friendly toward us. I never felt the stigma of discrimination here, not even one time that I can remember.

Desperately broke, and with more than a hundred thousand dollars in student loan debt, our family moved to Oologah. Dr. Maltsberger and his wife were kind enough to loan us three thousand dollars to use for a down payment to buy our first house. This was the American dream for us. Rachel and I were so happy.

In 1994, I moved my family to Oologah, and three years later, the Lord blessed us with another beautiful little girl. We named her Rebekah.

When we look back, we can't help but believe that it was God who guided our footsteps. God had His hand on us all the time, and we didn't even realize it. He was the one who brought us to America. He divinely orchestrated circumstances to happen on our behalf before we were ever born. Our destiny was set by God. The Word of God even declares that we are fearfully and wonderfully made:

> I will praise thee; for I am fearfully and wonderfully made: marvellous are thy works; and that my soul knoweth right well. My substance was not hid from thee, when I was made in secret, and curiously wrought in the lowest parts of the earth. Thine eyes did see my substance, yet being unperfect; and in thy book all my members were written, which in continuance were fashioned, when as yet there was none of them. How precious also are thy thoughts unto me, O God! how great is the sum of them!
>
> —Psalm 139:14–17

Rachel and I have learned that God knows what is best for us. He is still in the business of helping and guiding people to accomplish His will. He moved us to the place where He saw that it was best for us and for His kingdom. We believe that the will of God will never take us where the grace of God will not protect us. God wants to move through us and for us in the most personal way.

In 1997, we moved our dental practice closer to our church in Owasso (Owasso is an Indian word for "the end of trail"). Being a Cambodian-American dentist in such a little town has caused people much curiosity. One of my friends called me "a turtle on a post." I told him that I had gotten my tongue wrapped around my eye tooth and I couldn't see where he was going with that. He laughed. I asked him to explain what it means to be a turtle on a post. And this is what he told me.

"Once, there was a teenaged turtle trying to escape to the other side of the highway of life, for his side of the field was in great danger. A wildfire had burn his field and had killed some of his friends, relatives, and even his father. The young turtle managed to cross the dangerous highway and made it safely to the center median. Stuck there by a tall giant concrete wall, he couldn't go any further.

"Knowing full well that he didn't have the ability to jump over the giant concrete wall, the little turtle resigned to get himself back to where he had come from, but the danger of the highway became too hostile for the poor turtle. Feeling hopeless and trapped, the young turtle prayed that someone would have compassion to rescue him. He waited there with his head hiding in his shell.

"One day a kind old man noticed the poor turtle. He stopped his truck to rescue it. With the turtle in his hand, he jumped over the concrete barrier and carried him safely to the other side. When he got there, he put that turtle on a fence post. 'You can see much better from here,' he said."

I knew and believed that God had rescued me and brought me to Oologah for a special purpose, but I had never thought of myself as being a turtle on a post. I told my friend that I would be whatever God wants me to be to declare His glory and to share with people His good news. Everything I am and everything I will be is because of His grace.

With the Apostle Paul, I want to echo: "I am crucified with Christ: nevertheless I live; yet not I, but Christ liveth in me: and the life which I now live in the flesh I live by the faith of the Son of God, who loved me, and gave himself for me" (Galatians 2:20). I live my life to honor Him. I have nothing to boast but Christ.

With the psalmist I want to declare His glory and wonderful works.

I will bless the LORD at all times: his praise shall continually be in my mouth. My soul shall make her boast in the LORD: the humble shall hear thereof, and be glad. O magnify the LORD with me, and let us exalt his name together. I sought the LORD, and he heard me, and delivered me from all my fears. They looked unto him, and were lightened: and their faces were not ashamed. This poor

man cried, and the LORD heard him, and saved him out of all his
troubles.   —Psalm 34:1–6

I may look out of place, but I don't feel it. I feel right at home—sometimes too much—and I forget where I came from. Here is a good
example of that.

One spring day I took Rebekah fishing down at the river below
Lake Oologah. It was only two minutes away from our home. We got
there early—before sunrise. No one was there yet. This was our little
secret fishing hole. We were enjoying catching a lot of fish. Suddenly
a man showed up, making a lot of noise and disturbing us. He wore
no shirt, exposing his sunburnt red neck. His blue jeans were rolled
up to his knees. He was barefoot. He carried several fishing poles in
his right hand while holding a dangling catfish on a stringer with his
left.

When he saw me and Rebekah, he turned back and yelled to his
buddies, "Hey guys, there is Chinese here!"

I looked up and down the river to find the Chinese, but I could
not find one anywhere. So I asked Rebekah, "Do you see any Chinese
anywhere?"

Being a very honest child, she responded, "Dad, you are it!"

I was surprised by her answer, forgetting who I was, "What about
you?" I asked.

Rebekah looked at me really funny and said, "Dad, I am not
Chinese at all. I was born here in Claremore, Oklahoma."

Here is the truth I want to share. No matter what situation people
are born into, God can bring positive change. No matter how destructive the circumstances, God can bring about something better. Look
at me and where I came from. If God can do something with me, He
definitely can bring about something better with anyone.

I hope that I don't come across as being boastful. I am not. I am
no more than a turtle on a fence post, or a beggar who is trying to tell
another beggar where to find bread. I am writing this book out of my

grateful heart, hoping to share with people my passion for living the ultimate life in Christ. God has radically changed my life. I have seen his power transform our neighbors, friends, and many others who have put their hope and trust in Him. And each day I can't wait to tell people about God and how He can make a difference in their lives. The purpose of my existence is to tell people about the good news of Jesus Christ, that God has forgiven their sin already, and that they can live a victorious life. God loves you.

Chapter 8

Return to the Killing Fields

"I will never go back to Cambodia!" was what I told myself once I became naturalized as an American citizen. Quite often in my quiet moments, I have asked the Lord why I should go back to a country that killed my family, raped my people of their dignity, forced us to work as slaves, starved my father and grandparents to death, and deprived us all of our human rights. These were my bitter thoughts when I first arrived in the United States. However, after I met Jesus, my heart was changed and I became very concerned about the Cambodian people. But fear of the past still had a grip on me.

Fear was what kept me from going back to Cambodia for many years. I knew in my heart that the people of Cambodia were desperate and crying out for help, but fear crippled me. I had many excuses for not going. I tried reasoning with myself that it took Moses forty years to be ready to go back to Egypt. My heart was broken for my peoples' suffering. I knew what it was like to live under oppression, without hope. It was like being trapped in the bottom of a dry well, without food, water, light, and in agony, without anyone knowing. When I was a boy trapped in the darkness of my life, I used to look up into Heaven and ask, "Does anyone really care?"

Once I became a believer, I told the Lord that I would do anything . . . but please don't send me to Cambodia!

"Lord, I will send the missionaries over there. I will pray and financially support them, and when they return, they can come and stay with me in the missionary room at my house."

I also promised God that I would do evangelism and disciple people here in my town. I would teach, preach, pray, visit, make phone calls, tithe, and give offerings to missions. I would even go to Mexico to do mission work . . . but please don't send me back to Cambodia! I was afraid to go back. After all, my former enemies were still there. I had fled from them for my life, and now I had found comfort in my newly adopted country. So just like Moses, I reasoned with the Lord. I was very comfortable with my life, and I did not want to face my pain. I thought the past was too strong to face. The present was full of personal goals and dreams.

At this time, I was building my dream home. The Lord knew exactly how to get my attention. He used my wife.

One night I was sound asleep when my wife woke me up. "Bong!" (A Cambodian term of affection and respect, it's what a loving wife would call her husband or a younger person would call anyone in place of using his or her name.) "I have something extremely important to talk with you about." She was sitting up. I yawned, and looked over at the clock on the bedside table.

"Uh, what? Yes, darling!" I dozed off again.

"Bong! Can you hear me?" she pleaded.

"Okay, I'm up." I sat up and turned on the lamp beside the bed.

"I must go to Cambodia." Rachel said it as a matter of fact.

"Excuse me? Cambodia?" I was shocked.

She continued, "The Lord told me I must go to Cambodia." I was totally awake and alert now.

"You are my wife, a woman. It is not safe there. Don't you know?" I was rather upset.

"I know," she quietly answered. We sat there on the bed in silence for a few minutes. "I must go and tell my brother and my other relatives about Jesus Christ. He is the only hope for them," she pleaded.

I tried to explain to her what she already knew, "Cambodia is still one of the most dangerous places in the world. People are being kidnapped, land mines are still scattered in the rice fields and the woods, cobras are everywhere, and communists are still hiding in certain areas of the country. The political system is unstable. Contagious diseases such as malaria, hepatitis, AIDS, and dengue fever are rampant. One of my cousins had his head cut off by a young group of thugs who robbed him of his scooter!"

"If the Lord told me to go, then He will protect me," Rachel replied.

"I know He would without any doubt. Why don't we pray about it? Go to sleep, and get some rest." I encouraged her to go back to sleep, knowing that my sleep was finished for the night. How could I go back to sleep? My own wife was going to the Killing Fields.

The nightmares of the past flooded my mind, and I relived the scenes over and over again. The agonizing cry of my mother holding my dead baby sister in her arms. The bloody broken legs of my friend Pheng. The fall of the country into the hands of the ruthless Khmer Rouge communists. The exodus from the city to the countryside. The execution of people. Starvation, labor camps, separation of families, the death camps, the blood, the wounds, the sick and the tormented, the rice fields, the war, the snakes, the jungle. It seemed like it was just yesterday.

"It is just not safe for her to go there!" I repeated over and over in my mind.

I tried to find different ways to persuade Rachel not to go to Cambodia, but none of them seemed good enough. Finally, I told my wife, "I cannot go to Cambodia, you know. This is not a good time. We are in the middle of construction on our new home, and I need more time than this to close down the dental office so I can go with you."

"I understand. I will talk with Michelle to see if she is willing to go with me," answered Rachel.

"Oh, Michelle. Are you kidding me? She will not go. She can't stand the sight of a cricket or any other insect. She's afraid of a little ant! What makes you think she would go to a country that has king cobras?" I disagreed with her choice.

"Maybe she will go. It doesn't hurt to ask," Rachel replied.

"What about water? Michelle doesn't drink water! She only drinks Pepsi. Where can you find a Pepsi for her to drink?" I asked. Michelle, my wife's friend, had not gone out of the comfort of the United States in her entire lifetime. I didn't think she would go to Cambodia. If she did, then it would have to be God.

My wife made the phone call to Michelle, and—wouldn't you know—she agreed. I couldn't believe it! I reserved their tickets and they packed their bags with Tums, Tylenol, ibuprofen, Band-Aids, nonperishable food, sanitizer, and bug spray. They got all their shots, and off they went, flying to Phnom Penh, Cambodia.

My prayer life greatly improved! I was on my knees day and night, pleading to God for His protection for Rachel and Michelle. When they arrived in Phnom Penh, the capital of Cambodia, they met another Cambodian woman, Darnette, who would be their guide. The three women asked a missionary couple name Bruce and Margaret McKee to take them to Rachel's village, which was located about one day's drive from Phnom Penh. The couple agreed to take them, but warned Rachel that no missionary had gone there before, and it was extremely unsafe, especially at night.

The way back to her village was full of adventure. The road was unpaved and littered with potholes that could swallow a whole car. The dust in the air was so thick it completely blanketed all the trees along the road. When Michelle and Rachel got to Khnach Romeas village, my wife told me that over eight hundred people were waiting for her under the mimosa tree. They had been sitting on the ground, anticipating their arrival for several hours. They wanted to know why two women were willing to risk their lives to come to such a place.

Rachel had the people sit in two different small groups. She took one and Michelle took the other. There, Rachel, my beautiful, soft-spoken bride, shared with them the reason why she felt the need to come back to Cambodia. She told them that God loved them and that He had forgiven all their sins, and that He was not willing that anyone should perish but that He wanted them to have eternal life. On that day, over four hundred people gave their lives to the Lord, praying, and accepting Jesus as their Lord and Saviour!

Rachel was right when she told me that the will of God never takes her where the grace of God will not protect her. Full of excitement and joy, Rachel and Michelle returned safely home. That day, I decided that I was going back to Cambodia. I shut down the construction on our home, closed down the operation of our dental practice, and bought the tickets. On May 15, 2004, with my wife and our two little daughters, I flew to Cambodia for the first time since I left there in 1979.

Suddenly I had a sense of urgency in my heart to go to Cambodia to do mission work. And nothing was going to stop me now. No fear was going to hold me back. The Lord used Rachel to teach me to have the courage to step out on faith and to be bold for His kingdom. Rachel is one of those believers who sings "Wherever He Leads I Will Follow" . . . and means it. She is a woman of faith. She understands urgency when she sees it. She has the faith to act on it. Rachel demonstrated to me the true measure of success—to follow where God leads when others put detour signs in your path.

Chapter 9

Facing the Past

Now unto him that is able to do exceeding abundantly above all
that we ask or think, according to the power that worketh in us.
—Ephesians 3:20

On a Boeing 747 jet flying thirty-three thousand feet in the air on
the way back to Cambodia, I felt sick. The possibility of facing my
former enemy made me sick to my stomach. It had been over twenty
years since I escaped from Cambodia and came to live in America.
A lot of things had changed. I had changed! I was only a boy then,
and now I was a man, married with two daughters. One thing that had
not changed in me was the nightmare of the past, and I really didn't
want to face it.

While sitting on that plane, I was on an emotional roller coaster.
The horrific memories of my past haunted me. Scenes played over
and over in my mind. Those memories, along with the turbulence of
the airplane, made me nauseous. I grabbed the airsick bag, opened it
up, placed my nose and mouth in the bag, and breathed deeply as I
bowed my head forward and placed it between my knees.

"Are you all right?" My wife thoughtfully asked. My response
to her was that, no, I wasn't all right. I was dizzy, and any minute I
knew I would be spewing all my anxiety, fears, and nervousness right
into that bag.

"Did you take Dramamine?" Rachel knows that I don't do well on flights, and often get motion sickness.

"I did take the Dramamine," I responded, "but I don't think that is what is causing me to be sick," I moaned.

"You can do this. I know it is painful, but we can do it together," she whispered to me as she stroked my neck, massaging it. I assured her that I could do it, although it would not be fun. I sat up and looked at my wife and then glanced toward the seats behind us to check on our daughters. Mollina was ten at the time, and Rebekah was six. They were sleeping peacefully. Watching them reminded me of the scripture which I had taught them to memorize. In fact, we had these verses painted on their bathroom wall:

Trust in the LORD with all thine heart; and lean not unto thine own understanding. In all thy ways acknowledge him, and he shall direct thy paths. —Proverbs 3:5–6

"Lord, I trust You with all my heart. I believe that You are strong enough to help me through any circumstance, but now Lord, I am scared. I can't do it alone. I need Your help." As I prayed this prayer, another scripture came to my mind.

I can do all things through Christ which strengtheneth me. —Philippians 4:13

These are my life verses. I have stood on them as my foundation, and I have asked both of my daughters to memorize them.

Our youngest daughter, Rebekah, used to have a favorite saying: "I can't." Whenever her mother and I would ask her to do something, she would usually give us the same reply: "I can't." I used to ask her if she was not willing to do it, or was she not able to do it? I believe that most Christians are not willing to serve God because of fear. We don't want to get out of our comfort zone. Just like me. I didn't want to leave the security of the United States of America and go to a dangerous country. We trust God with our eternal salvation, but we tend not to trust His protection. Just like Rebekah, we tell God, "I can't," instead of saying, "Yes, Lord, I can!"

One day, all on her own Rebekah took a big, empty Folgers coffee can, removed the lid, with a black marker wrote the word, "I" on a white piece of paper, and taped it to the outside of the can. She then put her "I" can on her lamp stand next to her bed as a reminder that all things are possible with God. One time, she even wore the can on her head. I was so proud of her!

On that trip, I wore my "I can" on my head and heart for my heavenly Father to see, even though it was only inside my heart. He knew I was scared. I remembered something John Wayne once said, "Courage is being scared to death—but saddling up anyway." I was wearing my "I can" and saddling up.

The thought of Rebekah's can brought a smile to my face. I felt washed and refreshed and ready to see what God had in store for me. Right there the Lord taught me a great truth. There is power in what we think. Our thinking can build us up, or it can destroy us. Thinking affects our attitude, and our attitude determines the outcome of our journey through life. God, our Creator, knows how we are, and that is why He instructs us to think on the positive things of life.

Look at the advice the Apostle Paul gave to the Christians:

> Finally, brethren, whatsoever things are true, whatsoever things are honest, whatsoever things are just, whatsoever things are pure, whatsoever things are lovely, whatsoever things are of good report; if there be any virtue, and if there be any praise, think on these things. —Philippians 4:8

God wants us to dwell on the wonderful things of life, not on the garbage of this world. He knows that we can think ourselves to the point of being sick, and, most of the time, what we think about is not actually reality. It is fear built by our imagination. God, on the other hand, reigns over our fears and can "do exceeding abundantly above all that we ask or think, according to the power that worketh in us" (Ephesians 3:20).

The flight from Tulsa, Oklahoma, to Cambodia took over two days. As the plane landed in Pochentong Airport in the capital city of Phnom Penh, I anxiously peered through the window, surveying the landing field. The airport is small. It had only one runway, and at the end of the runway was a stucco building, which was the terminal. Along the side of the runway was a wide ditch filled with lotus plants with pink blossoms. Giant palm trees stood tall in the background. The last time I saw this field was in 1975 from the back of an army truck as I was being hauled away, along with my family and many others, to an unknown destiny. We were prisoners of war. The airport field then was full of ditches and giant craters from the bombs. The building at that time was torn apart and totally deserted. Cars and trucks were left unattended, burned to the ground. Palm trees stood like pillars with their tops cut off. The sight of the airport officials and the old familiar scene reminded me of my former enemy, the Khmer Rouge. Quietly I whispered a prayer. "I am in Your hands, Lord. Use me as You will. I am scared, but I know You are here with me. Your Word says, Even though I walk through the valley of the shadow of death, you are with me." With this little prayer, I stepped out of the plane onto the land of my birth and began what would soon be an incredible adventure.

Outside the airport, waiting for us among the crowd was our contact person, Bruce. His Caucasian skin, along with his white hair, stood out in the all-Cambodian crowd. I spotted him immediately as I exited the terminal. Bruce and his wife had been working as missionaries in Phnom Penh for quite a while.

The air was thick, hot, and humid, but people were wearing long-sleeved shirts and long pants. Some of them even wore surgical masks on their faces. I was thinking to myself how peculiar this was. I'm very familiar with wearing surgical masks in a surgical setting, but why were these people wearing them outside on the streets? Could there be an infectious disease in the air?

My thoughts were suddenly interrupted by many men in official uniforms running hastily toward us. With big smiles, they grabbed our luggage from our hands and carried it toward the vehicle. One of the men could speak a little broken English, "Let us assist you with your loads." I wasn't sure about the request. Bruce detected my uncertainty and said, "It is okay, Dr. Lim. Let them help you, and then give them a little tip." In no time at all, our luggage was loaded up into the Land Cruiser.

Suddenly I was surrounded by the four men crowding around me. "Bong, may I have some money to buy food," one of the men begged. "Sure!" I took out my wallet and opened it up, looking for a five-dollar bill to give him. All four sets of eyes were fixed on my wallet and without a blink, they extended their hands. I handed each man five dollars. They thanked me profusely, smiling ear to ear, showing their teeth. Suddenly, from out of nowhere there was a mob of men surrounding me, each one with an open hand, begging for money for food. I started to pan out more money, but Bruce came forward and stopped me.

"Get in the car, Dr. Lim, and shut and lock the door behind you!" I eased myself toward the door, but the mob was blocking my way. I pushed my way through while saying, "Excuse me!" and got in the car.

Looking out my window I could see the mob still begging and lingering near the vehicle. Bob put his Land Cruiser into gear and moved it forward.

"How much money did you give to each man?" Bruce asked with much curiosity.

"I only gave five dollars each, why?" I responded.

"Dr. Lim, you just gave them one-third of their salary for the month."

I was stunned by of how little they got paid.

On our way to our hotel I observed there were new construction sites along the road, but for the most part, nothing much had changed in the more than thirty years since I had left. The streets were filthy, littered with trash. The city workers, in their green pajama uniforms, were sweeping the streets with bamboo brooms. The traffic was heavily congested and jammed at every intersection. Trucks, cars, scooters, bicycles, and pedestrians were going in every direction. It seemed as though no one was paying attention to the traffic signs. Beeps and honking sounds reverberated throughout the city. I noticed that most of the people on the streets riding scooters and bicycles wore masks because the air was so dusty and rank smelling.

Beggars stood on many of the street corners. Most of them were women wearing ragged clothing, torn and worn, carrying an infant in their arms, walking along the street. My heart broke for them. In a war-torn country, women and children are usually victims. There is an old Cambodian adage, "When the elephants are fighting, the ants are dying."

People were struggling to get somewhere. It was amazing that there were no accidents. I admired their driving ability. The traffic was complete chaos, but everyone seemed to know what they were doing. One scooter carried six passengers—the driver, an infant on the handle bars, two little naked children behind him, and a woman sitting in the back with a baby in her lap. Incredible!

I asked Bruce how people come to live in such squalor. His response was that people here in Cambodia are survivors. They just make do with what they have. He reminded me that under Pol Pot's regime, the living conditions were much worse. People were starving to death. The elite and educated were executed. Most of the men died, survived by their women and children. The majority of the population of Cambodia was now young people under the age of thirty. Many international finance people were there to check on the possibility of investing, and to help rebuild the country. War destroyed most of the country, including the people. Most of the people living there now were children born after the Khmer Rouge. A lot of the women were left homeless.

"Wait until you get into the countryside. It gets worse!" Bruce informed me. He said that roads and highways were awful. Some bridges have only rotten wooden planks. In the rainy season, road conditions were very treacherous. Potholes and mud would swallow up the vehicles, and police would put up barricades along the road to stop people for tolls and "inspection."

"If you drive a Land Cruiser like this one, they won't stop you because they think you are a government agent. You see the symbol on the windshield? The Colonel, my friend, gave it to me to put there. It says 'Army,'" Bruce debriefed me.

Bruce continued to share with me that diseases were rampant, such as AIDS, hepatitis, malaria, dengue, tuberculosis, and parasites. He instructed my family and me not to eat any food from the street vendors. "Eat only fruit that you can peel yourselves." Bruce said that coconuts, mangoes, oranges, and bananas were safe. We were to stay away from the fruit that smelled like chicken poop called *durian*. "Talk about a bad smell!"

He said that homeless women and children live at the dump. "I want you and Ra [my wife's Cambodian name] to go there to preach to them. They are poor and helpless. I told you about them on the phone," Bruce informed me.

I nodded in agreement with his arrangement. I said, "I brought all the items you requested. They are in the big suitcases."

"Thank you for coming, Heng," Bruce whispered.

"No problem," I quickly responded with a smile, "And thank you, Bruce and Margaret, for being here in Cambodia, loving my people and telling them about Jesus." They nodded and smiled.

As we arrived at our hotel, Bruce informed me that he wanted me to meet an important friend of his—a high ranking officer in the Cambodian army—a colonel. He told me that he would come to pick me up the following morning at ten a.m. We checked into our hotel, and settled in for the night. It had been a long, tiring journey, and the Lord had kept His promise. He was with us all the way.

We should have been extremely exhausted, but the Lord's strength and power sustained us. Before going to bed, I gathered my wife and two daughters, knelt by our bed, and prayed to the one and only true, wise, and living God, thanking Him for His protection and guidance. I asked Him to give us strength and boldness to share His redemptive plan with our people. After we prayed, we locked the door with the dead bolt, put the safety chain in the lock, propped a chair against the door, and went to sleep.

Chapter 10

Church on the Dump

Come now, and let us reason together, saith the LORD: though your
sins be as scarlet, they shall be as white as snow; though they be
red like crimson, they shall be as wool.   —Isaiah 1:18

The Phnom Penh city dump was only a twenty-minute drive from the
hotel. The landfill was huge! I could see it in the distance. It looked
like a small mountain without trees. Several puffs of black smoke
rose randomly from the dome of garbage. The odor was amazingly
pungent. As we drove closer, the stench got worse to the point of irri-
tating our noses. The missionary and his wife took a couple of fabric
facial masks that were sprayed with perfume and placed them on
their faces. They handed a couple of them to us and told us to do the
same. They informed us that the smell would get worse. Even while
we were in the car with the air conditioning on and all the windows
tightly shut, the smell was unbearable. I wondered how much worse
it could get out there on the dump.

"How could anyone live here?" I whispered in the mask to
Rachel. As we approached our destination, I realized that the black
cloud I had seen from a distance was really a swarm of flies.

Rachel sighed, "How can any living soul live in such a place? It
is horrible and desperate beyond my imagination." Our hearts sank
as we saw people coming down from the mounds of trash, running

toward us. The missionary had informed us that this would happen. We parked the car at the base of the hill. Just before we opened the door to get out, Bruce said, "I'll keep the car running with the air conditioner on in case we need to get in here to breathe."

We opened the door, got our luggage out, and stood it beside us. The day was very hot and humid. There was no shade in sight except under a tamarind tree that was located about a block away from us. One block of walking on filthy trash is a long way! Two more members of our team, Piseth and Sokunthea, both new Bible college graduates, had arrived on a scooter. Piseth was a very soft-spoken, tall, dark, and handsome young man. Sokunthea was a pretty and vivacious young woman. The people came out and quickly surrounded us. Most were women and children.

The women looked like lepers, wearing clothes like rags wrapped completely around their bodies. Everything was covered except for their eyes, ears, fingers, and toes. Most of them had no shoes although some wore flip flops. Looking into their eyes, I could see only pain, suffering, and hopelessness. Their children stood beside them. Some were naked. Their bodies were filthy, but especially their fingernails, black from clawing through the trash, looking for plastic straws and bags for recycling. They were making their living by being scavengers. They had no place to call home.

When the last person came down from the trash mound, they all sat down in great anticipation, not knowing that on that day their destiny would be forever changed.

I took my mask off my face and proclaimed the Gospel of our Lord Jesus Christ. I told my people that my heart broke for them. I shared with them my testimony. I proclaimed the Gospel that God loves them and that He has forgiven all their sins. I told them about a new country called Heaven. I proclaimed to them what Jesus said:

> Come unto me, all ye that labour and are heavy laden, and I will give you rest. Take my yoke upon you, and learn of me; for I am

meek and lowly in heart: and ye shall find rest unto your souls. For
my yoke is easy, and my burden is light.   —Matthew 11:28–30

I proclaimed to them that they were destined for an abundant life, but
that the thief (Satan) came to steal, kill, and destroy their lives. Then
I told them how Jesus came to give them life.

I continued to proclaim the promise of God to them that they
could live in Heaven, but first they must confess Jesus as their Lord
and Saviour and repent of their sin. The people heard the message of
Jesus Christ for the first time, and many accepted Jesus as their Lord
and Saviour. Together on that day we worshipped the Lord with great
joy, forgetting for that moment that we were in the dump. Heaven had
been opened and light shone through the darkness.

Only a few minutes earlier, this group of people had only thought
of themselves as people of the dump, but, miraculously, they were
transformed into children of the Most High. They had been cast-
aways, but now they were treasures of the King of Kings. The garbage dump became the hill of Calvary that day. We totally forgot
about the smell, the heat, and the humidity. There was a sweet fra-
grance washing over us.

Vendors from the area came to investigate the event. Rachel and
I asked them to bring their cakes, ice cream, and water. We bought
and distributed refreshments to all the people there. We then opened
the luggage and began to disperse clothing, socks, and medicine. It
was at that moment that I got a little taste of Heaven. God was restor-
ing what Satan had stolen from me. He replaced my fear with faith.
He replaced my sadness with joy. But most of all, He reassured me
that I was saved for His purpose and His glory.

In the midst of the celebration, the missionary stood up with his
finger pointing to the tamarind tree and proclaimed, "We will have
church and worship God under that tree from now on."

What an incredible life-changing experience for me on that day
to witness such a miraculous event. The Lord must have heard their

misery and sent us as messengers. As long as I live, I will never forget that day. I am grateful that He used me to bring such an important message to the people at the dump. That night and many hundreds of nights after, I have thought about that day on that mountain of trash when God's Spirit came down and saved the most hopeless of those without hope. Each time I think about it, my heart is filled with joy.

Church on the Dump is growing strong. The two young Bible college graduates that were on our team got married that year, and they became the pastor and leader of that church. Pastor Piseth and his wife Sokunthea are still leading the ministry there. They have eight full-time staff working with them at the church. A mission team from First Baptist Church of Owasso has come along as Pastor Piseth's partner in ministry. The church has a feeding program providing meals for children five days a week. The city dump is no longer there. The government has moved its location. But the church remains there as a beacon to illuminate the ultimate life to people who live in darkness. Praise God!

Chapter 11

Taking Back My Shovel

Bruce let me borrow his Land Cruiser for two weeks. We picked up our guide for the trip, and with a lot of bottled water and food in the trunk we drove to Khnach Romeas, Rachel's village in the province of Battambang. This was also the province where my family lived during the Khmer Rouge's regime.

Our guide was the same woman who accompanied Rachel and Michelle on their first trip. She was also one of the Bible college graduates, and a friend of Piseth and Sokunthea. Her name was Darnette, and she was an orphan. She was around my age, and very petite, standing about four feet tall. But she was very courageous and boisterous. Her knowledge of Cambodia was extraordinary, and she guided us as skillfully as a GPS.

With great anticipation of what God was going to do through us, we drove out of the city. The smooth asphalt road quickly ended, and a rough primitive road with red dirt and giant potholes began. I drove slowly, trying to steer the truck to avoid those potholes. The further we got out of the city, the worse the road became. We came to a site where a bridge was supposed to be, but there was nothing there but two wooden planks. I stopped and wondered how I was going to cross to the other side. I saw a couple of local teenage boys waving at me from the other side of the river, motioning me forward to cross. Fearfully, I hesitated.

But Darnette urged me, "Don't be afraid. Go on, Dr. Lim; it is okay." My thought was that the planks would be too weak and narrow for the heavily-loaded Land Cruiser. Carefully and slowly, I drove the vehicle forward onto the wooden planks. Thankfully, Darnette was right. We crossed safely to the other side. Once we made it across the river, we stopped to thank the boys by giving them some fruit and water as gifts. They thanked us profusely.

Darnette told us that people here didn't stop to thank the boys as we did. Once they crossed the river, they sped up leaving the boys in a great plume of dust.

On one road, we passed by a shirtless little girl who looked no more than about three years old carrying a little naked baby boy on her hip and firewood on her head. I told my daughters and wife to keep their eyes on her. I backed up the vehicle to the spot where we saw her on the road, but the little girl had vanished. I stopped the vehicle, got out, and started searching for her. I saw a little path from the road that led down into the woods. I told my family to stay in the truck and wait.

I grabbed some food and a few bottles of water from the trunk, and I followed the path. Not very far from the road, I found the same naked little baby boy standing next to a shirtless man sitting on a dirt floor in an empty little thatched-roof shack. The shack looked desperately like the one my family used to live in when I was a boy. In the corner of the room were three large charred stones—that was the stove. Next to it was the small bundle of firewood the little girl had just carried in. The man was startled at my appearance. He stood up and asked me, "What can I do for you, sir?"

When he opened his mouth to speak, I noticed that all of his teeth were black and rotten.

"A little girl . . . I saw a little girl carrying firewood, and this little boy," I said, pointing to the baby. "Where is she?" I asked.

"She is bathing in the back by the well." He pointed to show me where she was.

I peered through the crack of the wall, looking toward the back. I saw the little girl bathing. She stood there soaking wet with a little coconut-shell bowl in her hand dipping water from a five gallon bucket next to her. She reminded me of my little sister years ago. My heart broke for her. I wondered if she knew that God loves her.

"What do you want with my daughter?" The man asked me with much curiosity. He had every reason to suspect my peculiar appearance at his home because many girls in Cambodia were kidnapped and sold into sex slavery.

I explained to the man that I was a missionary from America, and I had seen his little daughter on the road carrying her little brother and firewood. I had compassion on her and wanted to give her something special. Once he understood my intention, he was at ease. He called his daughter to come into the house. I gave her some fruit, clean bottled drinking water, and some money. I told her that another little girl who lived in a land far away across the great water wanted me to bring this money to her. The little girl was so surprised and happy. She received the gifts with much gratitude, saying "Thank you, Uncle." Suddenly, my family appeared. They had come looking for me. I introduced the little girl to my daughters and my wife. And then we told her goodbye.

We drove a whole day on this long, rough, dusty road trying to get to our destination. We still had another half a day to get there. Darnette told us that the only safe place for us to stay that night was at the hotel which was located in the city of Battambang. We arrived there late in the evening and checked in. The rooms were nice and clean except for the geckos crawling everywhere on the walls. My daughters were very afraid of them. We told them these were good animals—they ate bugs and mosquitoes. The place was secured with ten-foot-tall razor-sharp wire and armed security officers. It looked more like an army compound than a hotel.

We woke up to the sound of a rooster crowing at dawn. After we had our morning breakfast, we drove out of town to Khnach Romeas.

The road got worse. It had rained during the night, making it very difficult to drive, even with the Land Cruiser. Mud, dirt, and giant potholes were not the main issue as much as the little Camrys that zoomed past us at a hundred miles an hour. Those cars leaped like frogs on the road. Darnette told me that the mechanics in Cambodia put Land Cruiser suspensions and special tires on these little cars to make them drive like that.

We drove deeper into the woods toward Thailand. This was the path I had taken to escape from Cambodia over thirty years ago. I remembered that it was around here where a very large and vicious king cobra had chased after me. The communists had sent my brother and me here on a special assignment.

Cambodia was infested with rats, especially during and after the harvest. Some wild rats grew almost as big as a cat. My job was to kill wild rats. The communist leader said I could eat the meat, but he wanted the tails brought to him in the evening. He wanted to count how many rats I killed each day. He used them as evidence that I had been out there working.

"Rats eat rice," he said. "Anka needs you, Heng and Meng, to destroy them, or we will all be hungry again."

I was sure that this man was lying. We could let the rats eat all they wanted and still have enough rice to feed everyone in Cambodia. But at the time I was happy to kill rats.

Early in the morning while it was still cool, I left for the rice fields to look for rats. I carried a small shovel about two feet long made of steel pipe with a razor-sharp edge. Rats lived in holes that they dug into the dikes that formed the borders of the rice fields. Unfortunately, where rats lived, snakes also lived. The snakes ate the rats. And most snakes here are poisonous. King cobras, Indochinese spitting cobras, monocled cobras, and other poisonous snakes were there.

One morning when I was out in the rice field, I saw a pile of rice stalks about the size of six-foot-wide round hay bales. Rats normally could be found in such piles. I poked the pile with my shovel. Suddenly a huge snake stuck its head out toward me, flashing its forked tongue in and out. As it tried to bite me, I stepped back and with great fear took off running as fast as I could in a zigzag pattern. I stumbled a few times and fell down in the ankle-deep water of the rice paddy. I could still hear the sound of the snake chasing me. The rice stubs bent down as the snake moved. When I stopped, it too stopped. It appeared to be a king cobra, at least eighteen feet long. I was too afraid to move, so I stood still, ready to strike the snake should he come close to me.

He popped his head up to look when he was about twenty feet away. He moved his head back and forth. His head was about the size of my thigh. He was the biggest snake I had ever seen. He would make a lot of food. With one eye closed, I took careful aim and threw the only weapon I had—my shovel—at him, as hard as I could. He ducked his head down and started to chase me again. I had blown it!

Now the only thing I could do to save my life was to run. I ran as fast as I could, stopping occasionally to look back and catch my breath. My heart pounded like a big drum in my chest. I didn't want to die in the jaws of this beast.

After a while I could no longer hear the snake pursuing me, so I stopped running. I thought it was safe. Then I began to wonder how I could kill it. *It would feed a lot of people*, I thought. *But how can I kill it? If only I had a hand grenade or could burn the field. But that would be too dangerous. The whole country would be consumed, and Anka would kill me.*

I needed to get my shovel back. I stood there for a while, trying to catch my breath and gather my thoughts. Finally, I decided to go back to search for my shovel. I retraced my steps. The muddy water revealed the path. The shovel stood in the rice field where I had thrown it. I grabbed it and ran for my life.

So that's how I remembered my life as a boy growing up here during the communist regime thirty-plus years ago. I was scared, hungry, desperate, and running for my life. Now, with God's power, I had returned with my family to the Killing Fields to search for what I considered was precious and valuable treasure that was lost in the enemy's field. I retraced my steps. The muddy road revealed the path. I had come back to reclaim from the enemy what was stolen, and to take back what rightfully belonged to the Lord. This time, I came to step on the serpent's head. And I came to stake my claim. I didn't come to grab my shovel and run.

Our destination was only about thirty miles away from our hotel, but it took us about half a day to get there. We drove the Land Cruiser at a crawling speed in this rugged terrain. I could understand why no missionary wanted to come here. Along the roadside I could not help but notice that the thick dust completely covered all the trees, vegetation, and houses like a red blanket. Darnette told me that this was not even as bad as usual, because the rain had washed some of the dust off last night. She said that during summertime the air was full of the thick dust and people had to wear masks to get around, otherwise they wouldn't be able to breathe at all.

The air was so hot and humid. The car air conditioner had to work very hard to keep us comfortable. A few times I heard a groaning noise from the engine area. Sometimes I heard something loose rattling at the back of the vehicle, and I was very concerned. We drove slower than we could have walked. People were passing us on foot. The truck bounced and shook us from side to side like a pinball machine. It finally got us to our destination—Khnach Romeas. Rachel told me to go where the mimosa tree was, hoping that people were waiting for us. We were surprised. There was no one there.

"Where are all the people?" I asked and looked at Rachel.

"I don't know. Maybe they are at home or at work in the field," Rachel said, looking around.

Last time Rachel and Michelle were here, several hundred people were waiting for them. I thought no one had informed them of our arrival, but Rachel said that was not true. She said that she had told her family about our arrival plans. But the absence of the people under the tree turned out to be a blessing after all, as we were able to spend some quality time with Rachel's relatives.

We discovered that most of Rachel's family were believers, and many of them were leaders of the churches in the village. They were eager to learn more about the Word of God, and they asked us to teach them. We spent the rest of the day having fellowship, praying, and studying the Bible. We stayed there as long as we could, toward the evening, until they urged us to return to the city. They said that there was no place for us that would be secure enough, and that we must return to our compound before dark. We told them that God would protect us, but they implored us to leave. We relented, and told them we would return the next day.

The sun was ready to set when we got started on our way. At this time I wished we were on one of the smooth highways in America, where it wouldn't take us more than thirty minutes to get to our hotel. I ran into one of the potholes, which cause the Land Cruiser to jolt very hard. I looked back through the side mirror and noticed that the bumper had just dropped off the back of our truck. Out of nowhere, a woman appeared on the road. She picked up the bumper and ran away with it. I kept my eyes on her. She went into her house and came back out dusting dirt from her hands. I pulled the vehicle off to the side of the road and parked. I told the ladies to stay inside with the door locked. I was going to retrieve the bumper.

"Aunt, did you see my truck bumper?" I asked her in front of her house.

"What car part?" She pretended not to know.

I told her that I had seen what she was doing, and she still denied it.

"I'd like to buy it back from you. Do you have a bumper for sale?" I knew what she wanted.

"Oh, was that your bumper?" She responded.

"Yes, the bumper!" I took the money out from my wallet and

offered her five dollars. She gladly accepted it and ran quickly into her house and brought me my bumper.

I was very happy to get the bumper back and was anxious to get back on the road. By this time the sun had already set. I had to turn on the headlights to see the road, but the light was very dim. Suddenly the engine whined really loudly and stopped running. I put the truck into park and tried to restart the engine. It whined louder. I cranked a few more times, and the whining sound disappeared, replaced by a click, and then . . . silence. Dead! The truck was dead in a very remote area that people had told me was an extremely dangerous place.

I got out and popped the hood to see if the battery cable was loose. I shook both wires at the terminal. They were secure. I looked around to see if I could find help. Nothing was in sight. The village was in total silent darkness except for the sound of chirping crickets and croaking frogs.

Rachel asked me what had happened to the truck and I told her that the last jolt from the pothole had probably done it. She turned to Darnette and asked, "What are we going to do?"

"First, let's roll all the windows up and lock all the doors. Then let's pray for God's protection and guidance," Darnette suggested.

After we prayed, Darnette said, "Bong, I have a little brother who lives in Battambang. Let me try to call him for help."

I thought that was the best solution. We sat and waited with our windows and doors locked. I was expecting to see someone jumping out of the bushes at any moment. We were constantly looking around, making sure that no one was stripping off any more car parts. Darnette told us that it was not unusual for a vehicle to get stripped of all its parts in the night like this. "People will steal anything to sell," she said.

We waited a long time for Darnette's brother. I expected a tow truck or the equivalent to come to our rescue, but instead a tiny Toyota Camry showed up. Darnette's brother brought some strings with him. He tied one end of the string to the back of his car and I attached the other end to a hook on front of our Land Cruiser. I thought that this man had a lot of faith in his car. I expected to see the rear half of his car torn apart the second he took off. It didn't. He pulled, tugged, and towed us slowly, and brought us safely into the compound. The gate was already closed and locked when we got there. We banged at the door and asked the guard to let us in. As soon as we were in, the guard locked the gate behind us.

Darnette's brother came back early the next morning and towed the truck to the mechanic. After inspecting the engine, the mechanic informed me that the alternator was the problem and that since this Land Cruiser had been brought from America, there was no replacement part for it anywhere in Cambodia. He told me that the only way to repair the vehicle was to take the alternator apart and rebuild it. "It will take two days to fix this," the mechanic said. I nodded my head and told him to get started.

I waited there for the next two days, watching every move the mechanics made. This was a borrowed vehicle, and I wanted to make sure no part was missing when I returned it to Bruce. My mother used to tell me, "Son, make sure you return things to people in better condition than what you borrowed."

Two mechanics and two assistants worked full time for two days trying to attach the bumper and rebuild the alternator. Finally, they got the Land Cruiser running and in tip-top shape. They were hesitant to show me the bill for their labor and parts. I thought it was going to be very high, but when they handed it to me, it was only fifty dollars. In disbelief I asked the owner, "You must be kidding me. Is this how much it costs?"

"Is it too much, sir?" the mechanic replied with a guilty look, his face downcast. I informed him that it was perfect. I thanked him and each one of his helpers by shaking their hands and gave each one fifty dollars extra. With a great big smile on their faces, they showed me their gratitude by holding their palms to their foreheads and profusely saying, "Thank you."

With our vehicle now fixed, we went back to Khnach Romeas. During the day we made a visit to disciple new believers in the village. Through the night we had Bible study with the church leaders. We brought them back with us to the hotel. We stayed late into the night answering their questions about the Word of the Lord. Their passion to know the Word and their desire to follow Him were immense. The people there had very little, and they wanted to grow in every aspect of their lives.

After that first mission trip, Rachel and I returned home to America with a great burden and urgency for our people. We saw poverty and hopelessness at its worst. People were starving and sick, without medicine. They lacked basic needs such as food, clean drinking water, medicine, education, and opportunity. The infrastructure of the country was developing, but the progress was not fast enough. The highway and road system was debilitated. The security and safety of the people was compromised. Electricity was only available in the major cities. The educational system had not kept up with the rest of the world. Sex slavery was rampant. But despite of all this, the Cambodian people were eager to improve, and they had very open minds.

On that first trip, Rachel and I had an opportunity to meet with a colonel of the Cambodian army. He told me that Cambodia was in dire need of foreign investors to help develop the infrastructure of the country. He presented a list of twenty three items—roads and highways, a water treatment facility, a bank, oil and natural gas research and development, a hydroelectric facility, etc. We told him that we would like to help by sponsoring him to come to America so that he could personally meet with investors. We wanted to do as much as we could, but we had to stay focused on our main mission, which was evangelism and discipleship. Our hearts broke for our people. We wanted to help everyone, but the problem was that we had only a limited amount of time and resources. We couldn't help everyone in the country. We wished we could. At first Rachel and I tried to help them all. Each mission trip we went to Cambodia we tried to be everywhere, we stayed as long as we could, and we brought as much money as we had. But our time and our resources were never enough.

Knowing that the mission field was so vast, and that we had a limited amount of time and resources, Rachel and I developed a different strategy. We decided to go deep instead of broad. We can't reach everyone, but we can reach a few and develop a deeper relationship with them. We wanted to do more with the little time and resources we had. It was so overwhelming for us to see all the need in Cambodia. It was like having an elephant for lunch.

In addition to changing our mission paradigm, we also began recruiting other believers to go on mission trips with us. In the last ten years or so, we have brought many mission partners with us to Cambodia. Our mission team is focused on evangelism and discipleship, partnership with native pastors in assisting the sick and helping the poor, and educating the next generation. We build houses, churches, and do water well projects. Many lives have been changed. Many memories have been made. Each trip is special and unique.

On one of our trips, our mission team arrived in Phnom Penh, Cambodia, during one of the hottest summers on record. Cambodia was in the midst of a severe drought. There had been no rain for several months. Lakes, rivers, ponds, and wells were dried up. People had to walk very far to carry drinking water. Rice crops weren't producing. People in the village were without food. Our mission team had a truckload of rice shipped to one village. Widows, orphans, and people from at least a ten-mile radius of this village walked to get the rice. We gave them both physical and spiritual food. They gladly accepted both. Ninety-three adults accepted Jesus as their Lord and Saviour, and were willing to follow Him in baptism. But we couldn't find water anywhere to baptize them. They told us that they didn't even have enough water to drink, let alone for baptism. We told them that our God would provide the water, and that when it happens their pastor would baptize them. We left and drove to another province which was located a day away. We arrived there late in the evening. It was the same hotel compound where our mission team usually stayed.

It was there that we met a pretty, petite, teenaged girl named Srey (the Cambodian word for "woman") who was working as our waitress in the restaurant. Srey was the oldest of eight sisters in her family. Because of the drought, her parents' farm didn't produce. They lost everything. That was when Srey left her village to come to the city to work to support her desperate family. She worked at the restaurant seventeen hours a day, doing whatever was required of her including cooking, waiting tables, cleaning dishes, and much more. But the one job she truly hated was that her boss required her to sleep with male customers She told us that she had been there for a few months now and somehow she was able to outwit her customers by getting them drunk, and so far had managed to keep herself untouched. But she didn't know how much longer she could keep doing that.

"What are you and all these American men doing here in Cambodia?" Srey asked me while she was sitting with us at the bench outside.

"We come to Cambodia to bring the good news to our people, and these three American men are my friends," I informed Srey, and then introduced my wife and my two daughters to her as well.

"Where are you from, Uncle?" Srey asked me with a giggle.

I told her that originally I was from here but that I had escaped and gone to live in America for the last thirty years. And I had come back home to bring the good news to our people.

"What good news? I have not heard anything good in all my life? But your voice sounds so familiar," she said.

I quickly shared with her my testimony of how God rescued me from my desperate place and took me to America. She listened carefully. When I started to share with her the gospel, she stopped me.

"Wait!" She said that she wanted her friend to hear it also. She went and got him and together they came to the table. "This uncle has something wonderful to share with us," she said.

As I shared the gospel with them, the sky began to spark with lightning and thunder. The clouds above us turned dark. The long-awaited raindrops that Cambodia was longing for came and broke the long, dry summer drought. We picked up our dishes and silverware and scurried inside, where I finished sharing the gospel with them. After hearing about the love and forgiveness of Jesus Christ and His plan for them to have the ultimate life, Srey and her friend bowed their heads, praying to God and asking Jesus to come into their hearts. They requested that we baptize them. We told them that we would do it the next day after we had returned from our work in a remote village.

The next day our team travelled a whole day into the jungle to take medicine to the people in the jungle. People travelled as long as three days to meet with us. Ninety-three adults accepted Jesus Christ as their Saviour, and we baptized them in the pond which was filled by the rain from the previous night.

We hurried back to baptize Srey and her friend, but we didn't arrive at the compound until late that night. Early the next morning we came down to the restaurant and found Srey waiting for us. We could see that she was disappointed. We apologized and asked for her forgiveness.

That morning during our breakfast, the Lord impressed Rachel and I to bless Srey. After enquiring how much money her family needed to get out of debt, Rachel and I put the money in a Bible and handed it to her. We told her God loves her and so do we. I handed her the Bible and asked her to guard it with her heart. She received the gift with both hands. She opened the Bible and saw what the gift was and she cried. I had put the money in between the pages where Jesus said:

> The Spirit of the Lord is upon me, because he hath anointed me to preach the gospel to the poor; he hath sent me to heal the broken-hearted, to preach deliverance to the captives, and recovering of

sight to the blind, to set at liberty them that are bruised, To preach
the acceptable year of the Lord.   —Luke 4:18–19

We prayed to God for her protection and provision. And then we said goodbye.

The following year Rachel and I returned to the same hotel and asked for Srey and her friend. The owner of the restaurant told us that she was no longer working there. She had left around this same time the previous year. We believe that Srey returned home to her family.

Chapter 12

In the Nick of Time

A new settlement has sprouted up along the border of Cambodia and Thailand. This new village is found on the edge of a swamp right along the pathway which I took when I made my escape to freedom. I am very familiar with this terrain. In the summer it is hot, humid, and sticky. The sun is scorching hot. The ground is sizzling. When I was walking there, I could see the heat waves dancing on the path. It is so hot that it can turn a man into a bag of bones if he doesn't drink enough water to hydrate himself.

Wild plum trees are covered with so much dust that they look like terra cotta clay tiles on sticks. It was underneath these kinds of plum trees that I killed many king cobras for food. Here a man can drink several gallons of water a day and never have to urinate. He just sweats it out through the skin. In the monsoon season flood waters cover most of this place, and a lot of the road would be under water. When it floods, snakes and rats would come into the village taking shelter on higher ground among the village's grass roofs. In Cambodia when I was growing up, it rained rats and snakes, not cats and dogs.

Because the village is so remote and dangerous, not many people from the city want to go there—not even the missionaries. This village is what many would consider the end of the earth. The people there have limited access to resources, especially medical care. The villagers had pleaded with one of the house church leaders for help. There were many sick people in the village. In addition, many new believers desired to learn the Word of God, and they requested someone to come and teach them. After hearing about their request, I contacted a couple of missionary friends who were serving in Phnom Penh. They promised me that they would go to investigate, but after four days I received news that they had caught some severe skin infections on their way to the village and had to be hospitalized with IV antibiotics. Their entire bodies were covered with boils and pus. This unwelcome news concerned me, but I was still looking for someone else to go. None were willing.

After spending much time in prayer, my wife and I decided that we should go. I took my wife and our two daughters to the clinic and got all kinds of shots preparing for our trip. We packed eight large suitcases, each weighing exactly fifty pounds, filled with various types of antibiotics and other medicines such as Tums, Advil, Tylenol, children's Tylenol, triple antibiotic ointments, Pepto-Bismol, pills for parasites, and so on. With the heavy baggage full of supplies and the heavy burden in our hearts, we again flew to Cambodia. But before we went, we contacted a microbiologist in the United States and made arrangements for him to meet us in Cambodia.

On the way, the journey was uneventful. No airport officials opened our bags until we got to Pochentong International Airport in Cambodia. Usually, we had no problem going through customs. Most of the time our team would go through the VIP checkout. A friend who is a high ranking official in Cambodia would be there to receive us. Except that this time—the one time we needed him the most—he was not there. He knew we were coming. I had called him and confirmed our arrival time.

"Something must really be wrong for the General not to be here," I whispered to Rachel as we stood there with our children and bags. Other passengers went through the visa desk, got checked out, and walked through the customs checkpoint. None of them were stopped, but none of them had as many suitcases with them either. I thought to myself that we could get into a lot of trouble with this.

Rachel looked at me and knew what I was thinking. She came closer to me, held my hand, and whispered, "Everything is going to be all right." She grinned at me.

Speaking underneath my breath, I said, "You know we can get arrested for this?" She responded with her eyes, directing me toward the two men in their uniforms walking toward us. They were the airport customs agents. We pushed our suitcases toward them, moving toward the exit.

With a stern look on his face, one of the men asked, "What is in there?"

Cutting in front of me, Rachel answered with a big smile, showing her beautiful white teeth. "Oh, sir, it is medicine and clothes for our people."

"What kind of medicine?" Their faces lit up.

"Open them!" he commanded us.

"No, sirs! You can't open them. We have come a long way—all the way from America—to bring these supplies for our people. We took hours to organize and pack them." Rachel protested, still with a smile on her face.

They ignored her plea, looking at each other, their eyes rolling with sarcasm. They turned to us and bent down to pick up the bags. "We must open them and search," they said sternly.

"No, sirs, you will not do that. We have a friend who is in high authority. He knows that we are coming with these supplies, and he would not be happy at your actions," Rachel said.

The men released their grip on the bags and stood up, looking a little puzzled at what they had just heard.

I stood there watching my wife handling this conflict with such confidence. She was composed, poised, and friendly. I was very proud of her courage. She has changed a lot from the first time we met. She used to be stricken with fear at the sight of men in uniforms, such as policeman, or any kind of authority. One time when a police officer pulled her over for a minor traffic violation, she was so terrified she couldn't find her driver's license, even though it was right there in her purse. The first two years after we got married Rachel hardly said more than a few words. She was always very quiet and reserved. She told me that she was like that because of her past.

Rachel had a very difficult life growing up as a child in Cambodia. What she endured would cripple most people, but it didn't do that to Rachel. Someone once said, "Time heals all wounds." No, it doesn't. When a person has been abused, she can harbor an unforgiving spirit in her heart when she does not deal with that pain correctly. When she does not deal with it properly, given the right amount of time, her unforgiving spirit will sprout roots and grow into bitterness. But Rachel dealt with it the proper way. The Lord is the agent of change in her life. He has totally transformed her. The Lord is the one who gives her courage and confidence. The Bible describes her new life this way. "For it is God which worketh in you both to will and to do of his good pleasure" (Philippians 2:13).

As a baby in a remote village not too far from the one to which we were taking the medical supplies, Rachel was severely sick all the time. She had epileptic seizures, constant stomachaches, fever, and diarrhea, most of which I believe were caused by parasites, unclean water, and the lack of proper nutrients. Her parents told me that they desperately tried their best to find a cure for her ailment. They tried everything. They even consulted with the witch doctor, who used the cruelest forms of treatment. For her stomachaches, he burned her with fire made from cotton scraped from the inside of bamboo. Several people held her down while they put burning flames on her stomach. They burned her at least six times, producing permanent scars. For her fever, he scraped her skin over and over until it bruised, and sometimes even bled. For the seizures, the witch doctor demanded several roasted chickens for the sacrifices, which her parents gladly offered, only to find out that their baby's sickness remained the same.

In the end, her parents gave up all hope and followed the recommendation of the witch doctor by changing her name from Ra to Sunn. Finally, they gave her up to someone else to raise. The witch doctor tried his best to change Rachel's life, but he couldn't. Her parents spent their fortune trying to help her.

Ultimately, her parents did the best they knew to do for Rachel—they gave her to another family in the village. Growing up as a little girl, Rachel knew very little about what it really meant to be loved, but she had a lot of experience with what it meant to be a servant.

"In exchange for my food and a roof over my head, I served the family day and night. I cooked, cleaned, and washed all their clothes by hand. I worked in the garden, took care of their children, and gathered wood for cooking from the forest. I went into the fields looking for wild herbs. I fished in the creek. I was always alone. I never had any time to play like other girls in the village.

"My fondest memory was when I was occasionally allowed to see my grandparents. Grandmother was sweet and kind. She never raised her voice at me. But, unfortunately, that good time did not last very long. A bomb was dropped on their house and both of my grandparents died. The people that loved me the most were taken away from me. I hid in the forest and cried all alone. I wanted to go to their funeral, but I was forbidden to attend."

Rachel's life took a turn for the worse after the war began. Her parents came to take her back to live with the family, but shortly afterward the Khmer Rouge came and took her away to their labor camp.

The Khmer Rouge made life very difficult for everyone. But Rachel's experiences as a servant and as a gardener gave her an advantage over other children. The Khmer Rouge put her to work for them in a garden where she was watched by spies all the time. As a teenager, she worked in the garden raising vegetables to feed the village until the fall of the Khmer Rouge regime toward the end of 1978. That was when her parents came and got her, and together with her four siblings, they made their escape to freedom.

In the middle of the jungle, her family, along with many others, faced life-threatening dangers such as wild animals, land mines, and the most dangerous of all—the killing machine—the Khmer Rouge. Because her family had many babies, they had great difficulty trying to hide in the jungle. Her mother had a very young baby girl who cried constantly. Terrified of being exposed in their hideout, other people demanded that her parents kill the baby by twisting her neck. This is one decision that no mother should ever be asked to make. Rachel saw her parents do everything they could do to protect her helpless little sister. Her mother nursed the baby, and held her tightly against her breast to keep her calm. The Khmer Rouge did not find them. Her family finally made it to Thailand, where they stayed in a refugee camp. Although we didn't meet at that time, I was also there in the same refugee camp at the orphanage.

To help her poor family, Rachel sold candies. She walked around the camp selling candies from her basket. It was during one of her usual walks in the camp that Rachel was branded with her terror of men in uniform. The Thai soldiers who were supposed to be the security guards for the camp captured her, took her to their compound outside the camp, and abused her. They kicked her with their hard boots. They beat her with their fists and elbows as if she was a punching bag until she was unconscious. They stuffed her nose and mouth with sand. They pulled her hair. Her face and body were covered with blood mixed with sand. When she regained consciousness, they beat her again and again, and then left her there to die. Her parents found her and took her to a hospital in the camp, not knowing if she was going to live or die.

I was in the same camp, and though I didn't see with my own eyes what happened to Rachel, I saw the Thai's brutalities many times. One time I saw the soldiers shooting refugees. No one really knows why these Thai soldiers took their aggression out on the weak refugees. But whatever the root of their problems, innocent people such as my wife were paying the price. They abused teenage girls such as

Rachel, who did nothing wrong. These men in uniform instilled a fear in her that could have lasted a lifetime.

There are so many social injustices, pain, and suffering inflicted on mankind by others. Some people, like my wife, have learned to overcome and forgive the enemy, but there are many more that are still living in great fear because of what happened to them a long time ago. Rachel is a great example of what God can do when we ask Him to help us with our fear and pain. God has done an amazing job with her. Rachel could echo David's psalm, "I sought the LORD, and he heard me, and delivered me from all my fears. . . . This poor man [woman] cried, and the LORD heard him, and saved him out of all his troubles" (Psalm 34:4, 6).

The Lord has restored fully to my wife what was taken away from her. He replaced bitterness with joy. He changed her fear to courage. He changed defeat to victory. He changed her sad life to an ultimate life, so she wants to share her experience with others who are hurting.

So on that day in Pochentong Airport, Rachel confronted the ghost of her fears. Those two men didn't know anything about what she had gone through in the past. They were just trying to do their job. They didn't know that those suitcases represented life and hope for the young children in the villages. The medicine in those bags could save many children from getting scars and infections from burns on their stomachs, or from being scraped on their skin with coins. And this medicine might prevent many children from being taken away from their parents. This medicine might change the course of many children's lives.

In amazement, I stood there watching my wife defending the precious treasure. And just as I thought we were going to lose the battle, the Lord sent His deliverance to change our circumstances. Two familiar men wearing civilian clothes walked through the airport toward us. With great big smiles, they greeted us. They were our friends. One man was big and muscular, and the other man was short and very friendly.

The short man spoke, "Greetings, Dr. and Mrs. Lim, the General sends his regret that he is not able to be here in person to welcome you. His duty demands him to be away. Our country is at war with Siam." Then he turned to the men in uniform and asked, "Is everything all right?"

The customs agents smiled, scooted themselves back, and grinned. "Everything is wonderful. No problem." Our suitcases were released and we were free to exit the airport. And the medicine was able to be delivered to the village.

What can we learn from this? God can change defeat to victory. God is never late. His timing is perfect.

Chapter 13

Women's Island

The Khmer Rouge regime left many women widows and many children fatherless. In their attempts to rebuild their lives, many people escaped to settle in a new country; others remained behind. Some people have managed to cope with their lives successfully, while many are caught up in the abyss of hopelessness. A lot of people have had to subject themselves to many kinds of cheap labor out of necessity, but the most horrific one is in the form of sex slavery. Even though the Cambodian government has tried to outlaw this, sex slavery and sex trafficking are still in existence. Many children are taken from their villages with a promise of a better life in the city, but they end up in a brothel or working on the streets as prostitutes. This is an epidemic in Cambodia. I personally have talked with several people who have a loved one who was sold into sex slavery, or they themselves were victims of these ungodly schemes of men. But in the midst of this darkness, God has sent His light of hope to these people.

On one of our mission trips, while I was driving my team out of a village I saw three teenage boys in the rice paddies in water up to their necks. They did not have shirts to cover their upper torso. I parked the Land Cruiser under the shade of the eucalyptus trees, and walked out to the edge of the red dirt road, calling to them, hoping to give them some gifts.

"Children, what are you looking for in that dirty water?" They were timid in my presence. On seeing me, they huddled together, submerging their bodies deeper in the muddy water, exposing only their heads, and pretended not to hear me.

"Children! Do you hear me? What are you looking for?" I cupped my hands and shouted to them again.

"We are looking for food, Uncle!" the oldest responded.

"What kind of food?" I knew exactly what they were looking for. My brothers and I used to do the same thing when we were teenagers. Anything we could find—crabs, fish, snails, crawfish, snakes—anything that would provide a good source of protein for food.

"When I was your age, I used to look for food like you are doing here!" I shouted to them.

Once they heard that, they were more comfortable and they came closer toward me. "How old are you boys?" I asked them.

Again, the one who appeared to be the oldest responded back to me, "We are not boys, Uncle. We are girls." They were embarrassed, crossing their arms over their boyish chests.

"Really! Wait, wait, don't tell me. Let me guess your age." I pointed to the oldest girl. "Smile at me, really big." She did. I looked at her teeth. Dentally she looked about thirteen years old, but physically she looked more like six.

"You are right, Uncle." She acted really embarrassed, covering her face with her hand.

I pointed to the second one, "You must be twelve. Am I right?"

She nodded her head, glancing at her big sister.

I pointed to the third one, the smallest one. She had some missing teeth. "You must be ten. Am I right?"

She smiled and nodded her head. They swam closer but still kept their bodies under the water. I apologized to them, "I am sorry. Uncle thought you were boys, with your short hair." They still looked like boys. "How many sisters do you have? I mean, how many sisters are in your family?" I corrected myself.

All three of them said in unison, "Four!"

"Where is the other sister?" I asked.

With their faces all downcast, the oldest spoke with much pain in her voice, "Grandmother sold her; she is the youngest."

"Sold her?" I responded with disbelief. "Why?"

"To a man from the big city. Grandmother said she needed the money." They were all looking at me with very sad faces.

How can anyone have such an ugly heart that they could sell their own flesh and blood to someone? I told the girls that I was sorry about their sister and hoped that they would get to see her again. I quietly prayed for God's protection and provision for the girls. And after I prayed I told them to come closer to me so that I could give them some gifts, "Come here. I want to give you some money for food." They looked at each other, not sure what to do. "Please come. Uncle has no intention to harm you. Look, my wife and daughters are in the car."

They scooted themselves in the water toward me as I opened my wallet and took out some cash to give them. The oldest girl stood up out of the water, reaching up with her wet, muddy hand to receive the gift, while with the other hand she was trying to cover the upper part of her body. Her fingers were marred with dirt, her palm had a white leathery callus, and her fingertips were all wrinkled from staying so long under water. This little girl never had a chance to play a piano or stroke the hair of a doll. She and her sisters had lived a hard life. And for a moment in time, I saw my wife's childhood being displayed. My heart broke for my bride . . . and for these girls' suffering. These children are vulnerable to danger and to the elements. Smiling at each other, they repeated one after another, "Thank you, Uncle. Thank you, Uncle."

"You are welcome, but this gift is not from me. A little white girl from America around your age gave it to me to give to you," I informed them. "Take good care of each other, do you hear?"

"Yes, Uncle." And with that they crawled back into the deep of the water.

They had much joy in receiving such a little gift of love from God channeled through another girl across the world to put a little light of hope into the hearts of three little girls who were in great need of encouragement. In God's eyes those little girls are precious. My heart was heavy.

I felt a great burden for my people—more than I had ever felt before. I can't even write this without crying for those three little girls and the many other children who are living in such deep poverty. My eyes are full of tears. I am choked up with pain and anger mingling inside of me. The beauty of their faces is forever fixed in my mind. I am angry at the enemy who is responsible for their pain and suffering. I am angry at their grandmother who sold their little sister, probably into the misery of sex slavery. I feel their pain. But on that day, underneath the shade of a eucalyptus tree, my anger and pain were transformed to joy and gratitude for the goodness of God that divinely used me and another little girl as a riverbed to channel His blessing of love to put a little light into those girls' hearts. I was trying to savor the excitement of the recipients of the gift and of the giver.

I thought about the little girl who gave the money. I was preaching at a church in Tulsa, Oklahoma. There I told the people about the widows and the orphans in Cambodia. After the service, one of the little girls came to me with money folded in her hand saying, "Dr. Lim, this is my birthday money. I want to give it to you so that you can give it to another girl in Cambodia."

I promised this little girl that I would give her gift of love to one of the poorest girls on her behalf. She was so happy to hear that her gift would go to help someone in desperate need. The little girl gave out of the love of her heart. She heard about the need of others and she offered all she had.

Giving is an outward expression revealing the condition of people's hearts. There are many reasons people give. But the greatest virtue of giving is one that is motivated by true love. In high school I read a story written by O. Henry, *The Gift of the Magi*. It is about a loving young couple. The husband's name was Jim, and his wife was Della. The husband and wife each had one possession which they treasured. Della had beautiful, long flowing hair almost to her knees. Jim had a shiny gold watch which had belonged to his father and grandfather.

On Christmas Eve, with only $1.87 in hand, Della rushed out to sell her hair for $20. She bought a platinum chain for $21 as a gift for her husband to use with his watch. Jim went out and sold his gold watch to buy combs for his wife's beautiful hair. At home, both Jim and Della ended up with a gift that neither could use. But they also realized how far they were willing to give to show each other their love.

People can give without love, but they can't love without giving. True love leads people to do things that are unimaginable and beyond their normal ability. True love demands sacrifice when the situation calls for it, whether that sacrifice is for family or for country. On January 20, 1961, during his inaugural address to the nation, President John F. Kennedy led the nation by saying, ". . . let us go forth to lead the land we love, asking His blessing and His help, but knowing that here on earth God's work must truly be our own."

We live in a day and time where many people ask, "What is in it for me?" Or, "What can you do for me?" The entitlement mentality is growing and spreading among our nation. Instead of asking what others can do for us, people should be doing what President Kennedy said, ". . . ask not what your country can do for you—ask what you can do for your country." Until people realize that God has given us the liberty and the ability to make a contribution to our society, to make a difference in peoples lives, we cannot, and we will not, live the ultimate life. Life is not about what we can get. It is about what we can give.

Even nature demonstrates this truth. The Dead Sea is famous for not having anything growing in it or around it. The water doesn't move at all. It only takes—it does not give. Its water is bitter. In contrast, the Jordan River water flows downstream. Along the Jordan River, many kinds of animals, trees, herbs, grasses, and flowers are nourished. God doesn't want us to be like the Dead Sea—stagnant, dead, and not growing. He wants us to be a flowing river, a giver of life. Jesus said, ". . . If any man thirst, let him come unto me, and drink. He that believeth on me, as the scripture hath said, out of his belly shall flow rivers of living water" (John 7:37–38).

"Out of his belly shall flow rivers of living water" is an image of the overflowing, abundant, ultimate life that each believer is meant to possess. The Spirit of God is flowing out, and not just any kind of water, but living water! We know that water is the basic element essential for the existence of life. Water! People around the world are desperate to have clean water. People can survive without food for several days and months, but none can survive without water. Can you imagine that we have an unlimited resource of living water flowing out from us, and that living water is not coming from one stream, but many streams?

The imagery of a believer having streams of living water flowing from within makes me think of a great big river in Southeast Asia. The Mekong is the world's twelfth longest river, stretching twenty-seven hundred miles. It originates in Tibet, cutting through China, Laos, Burma (Myanmar), and Thailand, and then straight down south into the heart of Cambodia where it forks into two branches. The upper one turns into five mouths before reaching the China Sea, while the lower reaches the sea through a single river, the Bassac. The Mekong drains on the average 307,000 square miles of water per year. And it discharges 114 cubic miles of water per year. This volume of water could cover the states of Oklahoma or Missouri almost six times over. That is a lot of water!

In the middle, where the Mekong River branches to fives mouths, there is a tiny little island not much wider than a mile and not much longer than three miles. During the Khmer Rouge's regime, this island was used as a place of execution, or one of the many "Killing

Fields." After the fall of the Khmer Rouge, the government gathered all the bones and skulls and built a holocaust museum there. When the museum was moved to the city, the island was used for displaced people such as prostitutes and children. The local people call this the "Women's Island." There are about five hundred people, mostly women and children, residing on the island. These people are extremely poor. They live from what they raise on the land. The island is very primitive—no roads, no electricity, no stores, no kind of modern conveniences whatsoever. The only modern-looking building on the island is the church, which has no electricity. And the only way to get on and off of the island to the mainland is by way of a ferry.

A woman from the U.S. asked Rachel and me to look into starting a ministry on this island, so we gathered a small team and went. Our team walked all over the island talking with the people. Children on the island were extremely malnourished. Most of them were stunted in growth because they didn't have sufficient nutrients to grow. One six-year-old boy looked like he was only about two.

There was no school on the island for the children. Rumors among the missionaries were that there was a great possibility of arsenic in the well water. To find out for certain, Mike, one of our team members, took water samples from various wells on the island and sent them to a lab to be tested. Heavy toxins in water can cause harmful diseases such as cancer.

On the day we were supposed to give them the test results, our team arrived on the island early in the morning. Our plan was to walk from hut to hut inviting people to the church for the meeting. An old, skinny woman and a man who was supposed to be the pastor of the island escorted us. The woman looked very malnourished. Her eyes were hollow, and her cheeks were sunken. She had only a few upper teeth left, long and pointed straight forward like a duck. The man was fat. He was huffing and puffing and sweating profusely. He constantly stopped to wipe the sweat from his forehead. The old woman was energetic.

The village children, along with our own children, were following us. Along the path, children played with the plants that wilted at the touch of their hands. The leaves of the plants looked normal, but as soon as the children touched them, they wilted, withered, and folded, pretending to be dead. When this plant is left alone for a few minutes, the leaves return to normal. I told the children, "This plant is like us, wilted by the touch of sin."

We walked by three tiny huts on stilts outside the church gate, and the old lady told us, "The new women live." I couldn't comprehend what she meant, but out of respect I nodded my head, smiled, and kept on walking. We walked all morning until we got to the last few little huts located on the furthest side of the island. We noticed one particular empty hut, which looked all torn apart. The only thing that remained was the thatched roof. The dirt floor looked clean and well swept. We walked under the roof, taking refuge from the hot sun. What could have caused this damage? My first thought was a typhoon, but that couldn't be right. All the other huts were undamaged.

The old lady suggested that we go to the next hut and meet a woman with seven little children. She explained that this woman, named Navy, was very desperate and poor with seven little children to care for, but had no one to care for her own frail body. Each day she walked along the river looking for anything she could find to feed her children. Most of the time she fainted from exhaustion.

"She can't do this much longer. God has to help her."

Our team met with Navy. She was busy washing clothes and trying to hang them on a string. She was so small and feeble—as small as my ten-year-old, Rebekah. She looked as torn and worn out as her next-door-neighbor's hut. We visited with her for a short while and invited her to come to our meeting. The Lord impressed upon my heart for our team to pray for her. In the middle of praying, I felt compelled to give Navy some money. I opened my wallet to get cash, only to discover that I had only one torn, dirty twenty dollar bill left in my entire wallet. Like Navy, the twenty dollar bill was worn, dirty, and almost used up, but it still had its redeemable value. Navy is still precious in God's sight. I opened Navy's hand and placed the money there. She opened her eyes and I put my finger on my lips, signaling her to keep quiet. I did not want anyone else to know. We said, "Amen," and bid her goodbye. The only other person who knew what I had done was my wife, who hugged Navy and told her that she would pray for her.

While walking back, Mike came to me and said, "Navy looked so weak and frail, didn't she?"

"Yes, she did. Do you have any cash with you?" I asked Mike.

"Not really. Why?" He was curious.

"I am completely out of money. I have some in the safe at the hotel," I told him.

Mike said, "I just gave Navy some money, but I didn't want anyone to know about it. I have to be very careful not to hand money out. I don't want to play God on a mission trip, but Heng, I want to be sensitive when He tells me to. You know what happens when people see us handing out money."

Before our team left, Navy came to hug and thank us. I was curious about the hut next door, so I asked her about it. The information Navy shared with us revealed one of the truths which I have tried to convey here in this book: People who possess love are willing to give.

The hut next door belonged to the old lady that had been escorting us around the village. She was a very godly woman who had much compassion for others. Navy told us that, most of the time, the displaced women are brought and dumped on the island at night. The old lady leaves her home to minister to these women, cleaning their wounds, giving them a place of shelter and food to eat. But a few weeks ago while she was ministering to someone new, some mysterious people tore her home down. They carried everything they could away. Now she has no home and is staying at the church.

This saint is really living the ultimate life by caring for and loving others. Her life is "the streams of Living Water." She did not know much about church doctrine or theology, but she knew how to share her love. She did not have a house, but she had a home. Her heart is God's home. Maybe she herself was once a prostitute or a sex slave, but it doesn't matter now. Her value is not found in her frail body or her worn-out smile, but in her heart. She loves God where she is. There, a few thousand miles from America, my thoughts drifted to a quote spoken so profoundly by another great woman in another time, Helen Keller: "The best, most beautiful things in the world cannot be seen or even touched—they must be felt with the heart."

As believers, God commissions us to go to every part of the world to share His love. Maybe you cannot go for various reasons, but like the little girl who gave her birthday money, you can give. Or like the old lady on the island who does not have any earthly possessions, you can care for people. You can make a phone call, or send a card, visit a hospital, or pray. You can smile and greet people, showing the love in your heart. Jesus told believers they would receive power from the Holy Spirit to be His witnesses all over the world. The Holy Spirit has already come upon every person who has confessed Jesus as His Lord and Saviour. We are supposed to be His witnesses everywhere. We believers have the power within us to rescue perishing people by showing them where they can find the Living Water of our Lord Jesus Christ.

When the villagers came to the church courtyard, I was surprised to see many men coming also. Navy was there. So was the "Old Saint." People sat under the shade of the mango trees. Children were playing. It appeared that nearly the entire village had come. They wanted to know what was in their water. We couldn't use the church building that day. A big group of women from the U.S. occupied it. They were doing Bible study inside. The people in the village explained the rarity of a group of white women coming to their island. Since we could not use the building, we met outside under the trees.

A day before the meeting, our team met and discussed how we would break the news to the people. The test confirmed heavy arsenic in all their wells. The most difficult part now was informing the people. It was a very difficult decision for our team. The people were suffering so much hardship already, and none of us wanted to inflict more on them. All of their lives these people had never heard any good news. I didn't want to be the one to tell these women and children that they could die from the water they had been drinking. After much thought and prayer, our team decided that it was best for the people to know the truth. Our team decided that since Mike was the one who collected the water samples, it would be natural for him to be the one to give the report. And I would translate for him.

On that day, the sky was blue with no clouds in sight. Mike stood up and made his announcement, "Greetings! Thank you for coming to this important meeting. As you know, several days ago I came and got water samples from your wells. Do you all remember that?" Mike paused and the people nodded their heads. Mike continued, "Well, the test results of water in all the wells on your entire island confirm our suspicion. There is a heavy level of arsenic in your water. This is not good. It is bad."

The people's faces reacted with great disappointment and worry. They turned to each other and started to talk among themselves. I could only imagine how they must have felt to hear that their lives and their children's lives were at great risk from the water they had been drinking. Mike interrupted the crowd, "I know that this is bad news. Dr. Lim will tell you more about it." I felt so inadequate to talk to the people about this subject. In the silence of my heart, I whispered, "Lord, guide me in what to tell my people." I glanced over to Rachel and said, "Pray for me."

I stepped forward and said, "What Mr. Mike just said is true. Your water wells contain heavy arsenic. You must be very scared to hear that such poison exists in your water. Heavy contents of arsenic are known to cause diseases such as cancer. When you drink this contaminated water, you can see heavy, thick deposits of skin on the palms of your hands and behind your back where your kidneys are." They all started to look at the palms of their hands, and some pulled their shirts up, asking their neighbors to check their backs.

"From now on, you must not drink water from your wells. Don't use it to cook or to clean your food. Instead use the water from the river. But you must boil it first." I could see on the faces of some of the people that they didn't believe our report. I could hear them saying that the water from the well looks cleaner, clearer, and it even tastes better than that from the river.

Noticing that, I said, "Some of you are not convinced that your water is bad. That is your choice. However, the test shows the truth. No one really knows how the arsenic got into your well. But many scientists believe that it probably got embedded underneath the ground from volcanic eruptions several thousand years ago, along the Mekong River. You didn't put the poison there, and no one else did either. It just happened."

Without any warning, the clear blue sky turned cloudy, the wind started to blow hard, the branches of the mango trees shook back and forth, and the sky opened up with rain and poured down on us. The lightning flashed and the thunder rolled, but the people remained sitting on the ground. None of them moved.

At the top of my lungs, I shouted, "The heavy arsenic in your wells is not the only bad news I want to share with you today! I have news worse than that!" They looked at each other, wondering what could be worse.

"Each one of you has a well inside of you. It is called your heart. And in your heart there is a poison called sin. Just like the well water, none of you put the poison in there, but it is there. So is the sin in your heart. None of us put that sin in there, but it is there. You were born with it. Your parents and grandparents and their parents and ancestors had it. They passed it to you. Everyone in the world has it. The Bible says, 'The heart is deceitful above all things, and desperately wicked: who can know it?' (Jeremiah 17:9).

"The same Bible tells us, 'If we say that we have no sin, we deceive ourselves, and the truth is not in us. If we confess our sins, he is faithful and just to forgive us our sins, and to cleanse us from all unrighteousness' (1 John 1:8–9). Each one of us is born with it."

There on that day, in the rainstorm, the Spirit of God came down and touched the people on the island. People raised their hands up high to the sky, shouting at the top of their lungs, confessing Jesus Christ as their Lord and Saviour, asking Him to forgive their sins. What a glorious and joyful day to witness such a miraculous, life-transforming event. The people on the Women's Island found the ultimate life given by Jesus. They received the "Living Water." All of them were soaking wet. They were rejoicing with their new salvation just like children playing in the rain. The "Living Water" came into their hearts and washed away all their sin. This experience was rare, precious, and unforgettable. The island that once was the "Killing Field" was transformed to the "Living Field."

To help improve the conditions of life for our new brothers and sisters on the island, our team started a school and feeding center there. Mike and his wife, Liz, agreed to be in charge of the mission. They hired Navy as one of the cooks. They installed a water tank on the island and had water from the river pumped to it. They had a more modern kitchen built to replace the old outdoor wood stove.

When I think about the Women's Island, in my mind's eye I can see the children playing with the wilting plants. I imagine each one of them thinking, "Sin can make me wilt. Don't let it touch me."

The same woman who asked our mission team to go to the Women's Island also asked us to go to Cambodia to help teach workers how to minister to girls who have been rescued from sex slavery. There were sixty-eight women and girls at this center that were rescued from various places in Cambodia. The director of the center informed me that half of them had made a profession faith, but the other half had not. He said that it was very difficult for the girls to trust anyone, especially men, because they have been victims of men. The youngest one was five years old. Some of these girls were either bought back from brothels or rescued commando-style. They were abused, misused, and mistreated in every possible way. Most of the girls are about my daughters ages, twelve to sixteen years old.

That evening during the service, my wife and two daughters sat among the girls while I was preaching. I told them that when I was around their age, I used to live only about four miles from there. Life was very sad then too, and difficult. I told them how I saw many people abused and even killed. I described how my father had died from starvation on the bank of a creek just a few miles from there. I let them know that I too have experienced my share of pain and suffering. That I know what it is like to be hopeless. Just like them, I went through a lot. But I am not them. I can never imagine what each one of them has gone through being a sex victim. I know that they have gone through so much for being so young. People have abused them for their own selfish gain. Those girls carried a lot of pain in their heart.

I told them, "I have two daughters sitting here with you. I don't know what I would do if one of them would get abducted into sex slavery. As a father, I love each one of my daughters deeply. I would die for either of them. But, as much as I love my daughters, there is One who loves you more than I ever could.

"God loves you more than I can ever love my daughters. He is the King of Kings. Today, He wants to give you the ultimate life. He wants to make each one of you His princess. He knows about your pain, hurt, guilt, and shame. He wants to rescue you. He wants to forgive all your sins. He wants to give you the greatest life with Him in Paradise. The Bible says, 'But as many as received him, to them gave he power to become the sons of God, even to them that believe on his name' (John 1:12).

"God's rescue operation for you is this. He sent His Son Jesus to do the job. Jesus came. He was born of a virgin. He lived a sinless life. Because of our sins, He was crucified to pay for the ransom of the sin of the world. He died for us. He was buried, but three days later He arose. And now He is sitting on the throne in Heaven waiting for us. Jesus said, 'For the Son of man is come to seek and to save that which was lost' (Luke 19:10).

"Just like Baby Jessica being trapped in the bottom of the well, hopelessly waiting to be rescued, Jesus can save you from your sin and shame. Don't wait for someone else to bring you the good news. Today is your day of salvation. Will you trust Jesus with your life? He wants you to be His princess."

All of their eyes were fixed on me while I was speaking except one little girl whose eyes were glued on my wife. Rachel was holding Rebekah in her lap. I could see that the little girl was longing to be held with affection and love by her mother.

I finished my speech and asked if anyone was willing to receive God's forgiveness. Thirty-four of the girls came forward to receive Jesus as their Lord and Saviour. The little girl who fixed her eyes on my wife came forward as well. There, that evening, I observed God demonstrating His love with awe. With both arms, Rachel embraced the little girl as if she were her daughter.

She looked into the girl's teary eyes and said, "Today, you are a princess. And as a little princess, you need a ring." With that, Rachel took off her ruby ring from her wedding finger and placed it on the little girl's wedding finger. I couldn't imagine what the new little princess must have felt. But I could see the reaction on her face. Her mouth dropped open in disbelief. She cried. She reached out with both arms to hug Rachel, showing her gratitude with spoken words, "Thank you! Thank you, Aunty."

"Don't you ever forget! You are His princess." Rachel wiped away her tears.

Chapter 14

What If Dreams Came in a Shoe Box?

At about four in the morning, I was awakened by the crowing of a rooster. I opened the window of my hotel room and looked out at the city of Phnom Penh. The peace and quiet was only interrupted by the rooster. In the driveway in front of the hotel, Mr. Sin, our bus driver, was already up and dusting his fifteen-passenger bus with his rooster-tail broom. Mr. Sin was diligent. He had already opened the back door of the bus, getting ready for us. When our team came down with their heavy suitcases, he assisted us with them. Four other team members, including the microbiologist, met with us downstairs. After we had our breakfast at the local restaurant, we left for the village.

The trip was long and difficult, as usual. When the bus left the paved highway, it began to crawl on the dusty road that once again had potholes big enough to swallow an elephant. The dust completely covered all the mango, coconut, banana, and mimosa trees along the road. They looked like yellow blankets on sticks. It completely covered all of the houses along the road. It was like thick, dense, yellow fog. People who walked on the road covered their faces with masks. I felt sick to my stomach, and began to lose my sense of direction.

But Mr. Sin knew where he was going. He took us to my wife's village. Four men were waiting for us in front of the house church.

Two of the men were my wife's uncles, one skinny and tall, Uncle Saveth, and the other short and chunky, Uncle Theour.

After transferring some medicine into our backpacks, each one of us hopped onto the back of a scooter, each with our own driver. We wore masks on our faces and caps on our heads to protect us from the dust. Our drivers took us on a small path into the woods.

Uncle Saveth said, "This village we are going to visit has a small group of new believers. Your mother-in-law helped start this church."

The way to get there is treacherous during the rainy season. My mother-in-law has fallen off of the back of the scooter many times. One night, on her way back, she was caught in a rainstorm. Thunder rolled, lightning flashed, and rain poured down like a sheet. The path was slick. She fell down seven or eight times. Her Bible was all wet. The scooter fell on her. But God protected her and none of her bones were broken.

At the age of seventy, my mother-in-law is incredible. She loves the Lord with all of her heart. She comes to Cambodia about six months out of each year to do mission work—digging water wells, starting house churches, and training leaders. One year she helped dig sixty-two wells for the poor in the villages.

The other half of the year she lives in Rochester, Minnesota, where she works very hard to save money for her mission trips. She is retired, but in the summer she gets up at two a.m. to go corn picking for farmers in Wisconsin. I went with her one time. Her work is very labor intensive. She and twelve other people run alongside the tractor with a big trailer pulled behind. They pick corn in the dark field with very little light to see. When I went with her, it was cold and wet. She gets twenty-two dollars for helping fill the trailer full of corn. It takes one morning of hard work. During the day, she picks strawberries for the local farmer. She works very hard. To keep fit and healthy, she exercises every day. She normally runs five miles a day.

My wife is as devoted to God as her mother is. Both of them love God and others deeply. They are very passionate about helping the poor. They love missions. They go to the most remote areas in Cambodia where others are not willing to go. They understand what it really means to be sick, afflicted, poor, and helpless. And with grateful hearts, they are more than willing to follow Jesus to take the gospel to the ends of the earth. They believe that their mission will make the difference between life and death for these people. Both of them have found a new life with God, and they would do anything and go anywhere to share their experiences. I am very blessed to have such family members who are sold out to God.

Our scooters emerged from the woods and merged onto a little path along a small creek full of muddy water. The path along the creek was wide enough for a farmer to drive his oxen cart on. A few men and women were filling up the potholes on the path with dirt they had carried from the rice field adjacent to the path. When they saw us coming on our scooters, they stopped and stared at our caravan.

Their eyes were fixed on Mike, the microbiologist. "Hello!" they waved at him.

"Hello!" Mike returned their greeting.

It must have been a sight to behold: the first white man they had ever seen, wearing a black-and-white checkered cap backward, riding on the back of a scooter. Stunned, the people gazed at him. The path led us into a village.

Out of nowhere—and seemingly out of place—a very large, extravagant Buddhist temple emerged. The fence was made from painted concrete and beautiful wrought iron. The building was decorated with ornate sculptures on the wall and had a clay roof. Two stone dragons at least fifty feet high decorated stair rails that led up to the door of the temple. The temple was so big and extravagant compared to the surroundings and the shacks of the people.

We passed the temple, made a turn, and stopped where a lot of children were swimming in the creek. The children swam and dove in the dirty water. They cheered each other on to dive off of a wooden plank. Their dark skin contrasted with their white teeth.

We hopped off of the scooters, waving at them and shouting, "Hello!"

They waved back enthusiastically, "Hello!"

"Hello, children," Mike greeted them. The children giggled and shouted back, "Hello!"

They laughed and whispered to each other, "This white man is big and tall, and he has long nose." Mike didn't understand them. This was the first time the children had ever seen a white man.

Our team entered the house church grounds through a bamboo gate. We rested under a tamarind tree. I noticed a hut with four walls that had no roof. Behind it was a shack where the house church pastor and his family lived. The pastor welcomed us and informed us that the house without the roof was the future church. He apologized for his wife's absence. She was working in the field for someone and couldn't be with us. He brought some red plastic chairs out, set them on the ground, and invited us to sit down.

"It is okay, Pastor. We have been sitting a long time today, and we like to stand." Mike spoke and I translated. We stood under the tamarind shade, wondering if people were coming. The wet children from the creek showed up first, barefoot, soaking wet with water dripping, shivering, and with chattering teeth. Rachel, my wife, showed her concern by trying to dry them with a towel. Then women wearing sarongs and men in shorts begin to come out of the woods. All wore long-sleeved shirts.

Everyone wanted to see the white man. They had never seen one in person before. A teenage boy whispered to his peers, "Wow, he is big!" An older man spoke to his wife, "He is tall." A woman whispered to another standing next to her, "His skin is so white." I knew what they were thinking. They were admiring Mike. Cambodians have beautiful dark tan skin, but they want white skin. They would do anything to get white skin and long pointed noses. They put white powder on their faces, and they wear long sleeves to cover their body and hats to protect their faces so they can stay white. Tradition would require a bride to stay inside from several days to three months to protect her skin from the sun. They want her skin to be white and beautiful for her wedding day. I have actually seen a makeup artist use white powder to turn a tanned-skin bride into a white one. White skin is a status symbol, saying to people that they belong to a rich family and they don't have to work outside.

On that day under the tamarind shade, people looked at Mike's white skin, and they began to see the flaws on their own. They asked us to look at their skin. We saw a lot of diseases on the children's skin—ringworm, infections, and cuts. We saw parasites and lice on their heads. Every one of them had worms. All of the children's bellies looked big and bloated. Some of them had several scars. The adults looked malnourished and worn out. Their eyes were large and hollow. They work very hard out in the rice field with very little food and dirty water. Most carry some sort of disease. After interviewing them, the microbiologist confirmed that most of the people were infected with tapeworms and lice. He dispensed medicine to each person individually and saw to it they took it all.

Mike said, "The entire village must take the medicine, and from now on you must follow strict physical hygiene." He instructed each of them not to walk barefoot. He said, "The worm is transferred from eggs that live in the dirt, and they go through the skin of your feet and hands. It is important that you keep your feet and hands washed clean. And you need to wear shoes."

One old lady asked, "What are symptoms of a tapeworm?" Mike explained to them, and they hung on every word. For many generations, they had not known how disease spreads.

Mike is a very humble and loving man. He hugged every child despite the dirt, cuts, lice, and skin diseases they carried. The people loved him. He said, "Jesus loves you. I am not a good representative of white people though. They are better looking than I am. Next time I will bring my wife. She is much better looking than me." The people laughed.

As I stood there next to this devoted follower of Jesus Christ, I couldn't help but notice how humble he was. I was reminded of a scripture that says, ". . . How beautiful are the feet of them that preach the gospel of peace, and bring glad tidings of good things!" (Roman 10:15).

Mike may feel inadequate to represent his people, but he was doing a beautiful thing in his love to represent the Lord as His missionary. He chose the treasure that lasts. He was willing to leave the comfort of his home to come to such a place. Mike sings, "Go, tell it on the mountain, over the hill and everywhere," and really means it. And Rachel looked so happy to see that these children received medical care with the medicine we brought all the way from America.

Under the shade of the cathedral tamarind tree, with the sky open wide into Heaven, we worshipped the Lord by loving and dispensing medicine to the people. They gladly received it like manna from Heaven. They listened carefully to the instructions on how to prevent and get rid of diseases. They listened to us sharing about the eternal life they can find in Jesus. Many of them made decisions to receive the Lord. We read and studied the Word of God together, learning about the will of God for our lives.

After we studied the Bible together, I sat down and interviewed the children. Someone from America asked me to find out what the children in the village would like. I asked the boys and the girls the same question, "If dreams came in a shoe box, what you would wish to have?"

A brave boy answered me first. "If dreams can come in a box, I would like to have a notebook, pencils, and pens." As poor as they are, you would imagine that they would wish to have money, food, clean water, or toys. But instead they wished for basic school items. They want education. They believe that education will help them get out of poverty. They know that people are perishing for lack of knowledge. A girl wished to have the same things as the boy.

"What else?" I asked them.

One of the girls spoke, "If possible, we would like shoes, rulers, and an umbrella for a rainy day, and a doll to play with."

One brave boy spoke up, "We want a soccer ball or a volley ball, and that is all."

I went from village to village meeting hundreds and thousands of children. I asked them all the same question. To my amazement, they all gave me the same answer. They want the basic essentials for education. That is not too much to ask. So I asked those children, "Why do you want notebooks, pens, and pencils?"

Again all of them gave me the same answer. "I want to learn."

I probed deeper to find their reason. "Why and what do you want to learn?" The children told me that their education would take them out of poverty. They want to learn English so they can go to America, like me.

"I understand your desire to learn and to go to America. When I was young like you, I wanted the same thing," I told them. "I can bring you the school supplies, but unfortunately I can't take you back to America with me. I wish I could."

One of the girls asked me, "How did you get to go to America, Uncle?"

I explained to her, "When I was a boy, I escaped from Cambodia to seek asylum in another country. People in America had compassion on my family. They sponsored us and took us there."

One of the boys stood up and spoke for the group, "We want to escape and seek asylum. Can you find a sponsor for us?" These children had no hope. They wanted to find a way out.

I explained, "There are many wonderful people in America that have compassion on young children. They would love to help. However, the government has special laws that make it very difficult for people to go there." I told them that as great as America is, there is a much better place for them. People call this place Heaven. I told them about this beautiful place and what it is made from. I read from the Bible where it says, "And the foundations of the wall of the city were garnished with all manner of precious stones. . . . And the twelve gates were twelve pearls; every several gate was of one pearl: and the street of the city was pure gold, as it were transparent glass" (Revelation 21:19, 21). I tell them that in that city, ". . . God shall wipe away all tears from their eyes; and there shall be no more death, neither sorrow, nor crying, neither shall there be any more pain: for the former things are passed away" (Revelation 21:4).

I also explained that the owner of this great city is willing to sponsor each one of them, and His Son's name is Jesus. I shared with them the gospel of Jesus Christ and invited them to receive His offer. On that day seventy-three people accepted Christ as their Saviour. We baptized them in the creek—the same one that my brothers and I used to swim and dive in when we were teenagers. We used to work in the rice paddies just a few blocks from that creek. It is a very small world.

Chapter 15

A Wife Instead of an Inheritance

While in Cambodia, I met a man who had three sons. When the oldest son turned seven years of age, the father sent him to live in the city with his rich uncle. Having no son, the uncle loved his nephew as his own and eventually adopted him as his own son. The rich uncle did his best to raise his adopted son to be a man of character and intellect. He had a special plan for his son when he became a grown man. When the young man grew up, he went to medical school and met a girl with whom he fell madly in love. His father disagreed with his choice, and warned him to discontinue the relationship with her. His father said, "I have a special plan for you, my son. Wait until after medical school and I will reveal it to you."

Being an impatient young man who was madly in love, the son disobeyed his father and married his sweetheart after both of them graduated from medical school. Without any blessing, the son left his father's mansion to start his own home in a village far away. He and his new wife moved out of the city and built their own shack on the curb by the highway. This would later be the same highway that would lead him straight back home to his father.

The house was very primitive. It had no running water or electricity, and no modern conveniences. It was built on eight stilts above the smelly swamp water, with the front side connected to the curb of the highway. The roof was made from rusted tin metal. The side was covered with rotten wooden planks with holes, allowing the sunlight and air to pass through. The floor was covered with the same rough wood with holes everywhere. One could see the vegetation of the swamp water underneath, and one could smell the rotten odor of the sewage from the swamp. This was where the young couple lived and practiced family medicine, caring for the sick in the village. They were trying to make ends meet every day.

The young man had made a decision to ignore his father by marrying his girlfriend rather than finding out the great plan that his father had for him. He could have had a modern, state-of-the-art medical clinic. He could have held a high position among his peers in a famous hospital that his father would have built in the city. There are so many possibilities that "could have been." He would never know what his father's great plan would have been. He never asked him what it was. He didn't seem to care. At that time in his life, the most precious thing to him was his woman.

Do you know anyone who has made such a drastic decision? Do you know anyone who has run away from home? The young doctor made one decision that would forever change the course of his life. Studies have indicated that all of us have made hundreds of small decisions in our life, but we make only a few big choices. Choice of spouse, choice of occupation, choice of residence, and choice of faith are very important. And any one of these choices can change the direction of our life. Most of our decisions are small and insignificant, but once in a while, we make a choice that can cause a change for a lifetime. We have all the privilege to make our choices, but none of us can choose the consequences that come with each decision we make.

All of us are like the young doctor. We make our decisions based on what we believe is right in our own eyes, but sometimes our vision is very shortsighted; we can't see far enough ahead. We may make many mistakes along the way that cause much pain. When it comes to our eternal life, none of us can afford to make any mistakes. We must consult with someone who has great and everlasting wisdom: God. The Bible says, "For the turning away of the simple shall slay them, and the prosperity of fools shall destroy them. But whoso hearkeneth unto me [God] shall dwell safely, and shall be quiet from fear of evil" (Proverbs 1:32–33).

Rachel and I had the privilege of meeting the young doctor. He is my cousin. This was the first time in our lives that we had ever met. War has a tendency to separate family members like this. When I came to America at the age of sixteen, Sam, my cousin, who is much younger than I am, stayed behind in Cambodia, where he had the extremely rare privilege of attending medical school at a time when most young Cambodian people were living in impoverished conditions and working in the rice paddies.

When Rachel and I met up with Sam and his wife, they had a very cute baby boy, about twelve months old. He had the most handsome brown eyes to match his cute, chubby cheeks. He was healthy and very loving. He loved his daddy, and his daddy loved him. The two were inseparable. His daddy tossed his boy up in the air and carefully caught him as they both laughed.

Kim was the little boy's name. Rachel and I held him in our arms and had a wonderful time with him. Rachel admired him. "Kim, you are so cute. I could take you home with me," she teased. The child's parents thought she was serious, and they offered their son to us by saying, "Cousins, please take our son with you. We will give Kim to you."

"Seriously? No cousins, we were joking," my wife responded with a gentle smile, but they were serious.

It was then that I jumped in, "Cousin, that is very kind of you to offer us your son. He is so handsome. Rachel and I have two daughters, and we would love to have a son, especially one like Kim, who is my flesh and blood. But we can't take him. He is your son, especially the first and only one you have." Both my cousins had adamantly made up their minds to give us their boy. "Take him, please," they begged us, "and raise him as your son!" the wife pleaded.

Finally I asked Sam, "Why are you so eager to offer us your son, Cousin?" The answer they offered us is the answer that every loving parent would echo: "We want what is best for our child." I believe all parents, down deep inside their hearts, want what is best for their children. It is the same with our Heavenly Father.

Jesus said, ". . . What man is there of you, whom if his son ask bread, will he give him a stone? Or if he ask a fish, will he give him a serpent? If ye then, being evil, know how to give good gifts unto your children, how much more shall your Father which is in heaven give good things to them that ask him?" (Matthew 7:9–11).

God wants to offer us the ultimate life. His desire for us is perfect. The Bible declares, "[God's] way is perfect: the word of the Lord is tried: he is a buckler to all those that trust in him" (Psalm 18:30).

It's hard to fathom that God, who is perfect in every way, desires to adopt us into His family. What kind of a life does He want to offer us? The answer to that question is nothing less than His ultimate best. Listen to the invitation He offers: "Ho, every one that thirsteth, come ye to the waters, and he that hath no money; come ye, buy, and eat; yea, come, buy wine and milk without money and without price" (Isaiah 55:1). The Lord declares an invitation to everyone who is spiritually thirsty to come to the water and drink.

God extends the invitation, but people have to be willing to accept it. Jesus explains it this way in the New Testament. "Blessed are they which do hunger and thirst after righteousness: for they shall be filled" (Matthew 5:6).

Jesus later explained God's invitation to the ultimate life in this story.

> Then said he unto him, A certain man made a great supper, and
> bade many: And sent his servant at supper time to say to them that

were bidden, Come; for all things are now ready. And they all with one consent began to make excuse. The first said unto him, I have bought a piece of ground, and I must needs go and see it: I pray thee have me excused. And another said, I have bought five yoke of oxen, and I go to prove them: I pray thee have me excused. And another said, I have married a wife, and therefore I cannot come. So that servant came, and shewed his lord these things. Then the master of the house being angry said to his servant, Go out quickly into the streets and lanes of the city, and bring in hither the poor, and the maimed, and the halt, and the blind. And the servant said, Lord, it is done as thou hast commanded, and yet there is room. And the lord said unto the servant, Go out into the highways and hedges, and compel them to come in, that my house may be filled. For I say unto you, That none of those men which were bidden shall taste of my supper. —Luke 14:16–24

Can you imagine being invited to a royal wedding? Would you refuse to attend? We can never imagine what God's banquet really looks like. But we have a glimpse by looking at a royal banquet. According to Wikipedia, Prince William, Duke of Cambridge, and Catherine Middleton got married on April 29, 2011, in London. TV audiences peaked at 26.3 million viewers, with a total of 36.2 million watching part of the coverage. Over five thousand street parties were held throughout the United Kingdom, and one million people lined the route between Westminster Abbey and Buckingham Palace. Seventy-two million watched on the YouTube Royal Channel. The Australian newspaper, the *Herald Sun,* estimated $32 million was spent for security and $800,000 for flowers. More than half of the guests attending the wedding were family and friends of the couple. The rest were dignitaries.

As extravagant as this banquet was, the Lord's banquet for believers is far more extravagant than any words can describe. And the most wonderful thing is that the Lord has extended an invitation to His royal banquet to everyone who is willing to accept. God has prepared the banquet, and He has already sent out His personal invitation. Will you accept it? He knows that there are a lot of people with empty, meaningless lives, and He wants to satisfy that void. Listen to God's Word regarding His thoughts toward us. "For my thoughts are not your thoughts, neither are your ways my ways . . ." (Isaiah 55:8).

Any life apart from God is not the best; therefore, every thought we have would lead to self-motivation or self-ambition. This process of life without God can only lead to destruction. The Bible clearly states this path of destiny as "a way which seemeth right unto a man, but the end thereof are the ways of death" (Proverbs 14:12).

Truthfully speaking, apart from God we are on our way to doom. God is the only way out for us. The Bible says: "For God so loved the world, that he gave his only begotten Son, that whosoever believeth in him should not perish, but have everlasting life" (John 3:16).

God wants to restore our broken relationship. I believe that all problems in the world are caused by a broken relationship between God and man. The only way for God to restore people fully is to have the broken relationship reconciled.

I was wondering if my cousin had even put any thought into the decision he made that was contrary to his father's wish. My cousin's words continued to echo in my head as I travelled through Cambodia. "We want what is best for our child. Take our child with you to the U.S. You can offer better opportunities for him."

I assured my cousins that America does offer better opportunities for those who are willing to put forth the effort. But, opportunities are nothing unless people are willing to seize them. I continued to enlighten them that, yes, America is the greatest country in the world, but not all people who live there are successful. Americans have problems like anyone else, such as unemployment, homelessness, and financial, social, and spiritual issues. There are many refugees from many countries that have escaped their homeland to come to America in the hope that their children would have a better life than they did. Some of them do have a better life, but others face new problems, such as gangs and illegal activities. The parents had hoped for a better life for their children, but it doesn't always turn out in the best of circumstances. Some have taken their new opportunities for granted. They only want to have fun. Some parents make the mistake of spoiling them and giving them their heart's desires. There are those who are very diligent. However, many are not. There is a new generation who are into the new things such as computers, iPads, iPhones, video games, movies, music, sports, and the latest fads. They spend a lot of time with these new activities but forget the most important things, such as education, discipline, family, and faith.

I told my cousins that I would take their son Kim in a heartbeat, although the very best place for him would be with his loving parents. Even if we had brought little Kim back with us to the United States, what guarantee would there be that he would have success? Location does not change a man. Unfortunately there are those who disagree and have put their trust in people by paying thousands of dollars in the hope that their loved ones would get a chance to come to America. This is called human trafficking.

Several years ago in Seattle, Washington, a dozen Asians were found in the bottom of a cargo container. They were suffocating and lying in their own feces. They were sick, malnourished, and on the verge of death. These people, when found, were deported back to their country. In Florida, the U.S. Coast Guard found many people on a makeshift boat attempting to cross the ocean so that they could find a better opportunity here in America. Most of them had drowned. They didn't make it, but they had thought to themselves, *If only I could get to America, then all my dreams would come true. Then I would have the ultimate life.*

America can indeed offer a better life than any other place in the world, but the ultimate life can only be found in having a relationship with God. For those people who don't have that relationship with Him, they just exist. The bottom line is that the storm is coming regardless of who you are. You had better be prepared to change, because when the storm of life comes, it will be too late to prepare.

Chapter 16

Rise Above the Storm

Super Storm Sandy hit the eastern part of the United States of America just before the presidential election of 2012. Reports stated that more than six million people were left in darkness. Water flooded buildings, roads, railways, and homes. Twenty thousand flights were cancelled. Telephone poles snapped like toothpicks. Sandy left millions of people in devastation, and their homes were demolished. It appeared that Super Storm Sandy emerged out of nowhere and brought her destruction with her with little warning. The force of the storm was so overwhelming, there was nothing anyone could do to prepare themselves to face her ugly tirade.

In a way, that's how it is with the storms of life. Without much warning, we find ourselves caught in the eye of the storm. Such was the case for the people of Newtown, Connecticut. A twenty-year-old gunman shot his own mother in the head four times before going to an elementary school and killing twenty-six people. He shot twenty children and six adults. The gunman asked one of his victims, "Do you believe in God?" She said, "Yes!" And without conscience, he shot her in the head. Such horrendous actions have caused people to ask questions like, "Where is God?" and "Why does God allow innocent people to suffer?"

What happened to the people at Newtown, Connecticut, was heart-wrenching and devastating. Americans are still mourning the loss of those children and teachers. That sudden act of violence has rocked the foundation of our nation. And we find ourselves troubled by this storm. Sometimes when we are in the middle of the storm of life, it is very difficult to see the sunshine. We even question God and wonder if He is still in control.

At times we may forget that He is the Sovereign One, and that He has the ultimate power. God will not allow circumstances to happen to His children without His permission. Our God is all-knowing. Nothing can surprise Him. There is no "oops" in His vocabulary. Not only does He know everything, but He can do all things. He causes circumstances to happen, and He can change circumstances at any time.

The Bible says that Jesus is God and He has the supreme power.

> Who is the image of the invisible God, the firstborn of every crea-
> ture: For by him were all things created, that are in heaven, and
> that are in earth, visible and invisible, whether they be thrones, or
> dominions, or principalities, or powers: all things were created by
> him, and for him: And he is before all things, and by him all things
> consist.   —Colossians 1:15–17

In other words, the world is under His supreme command. At times it seems that it is not, but be assured that He is in total control. Knowing that this fact is true brings us peace. Peace is not the absence of conflict, but the sense of tranquility in the middle of the storm. Jesus said, "Peace I leave with you, my peace I give unto you: not as the world giveth, give I unto you. Let not your heart be troubled, neither let it be afraid" (John 14:27).

God knows that our hearts can be troubled and overwhelmed with fear and doubts. He wants to reassure us that we can live in peace in the middle of the storm. As much as mankind wants to believe that there is a utopia somewhere in this world, the fact is, there isn't one. This world in which we live is full of surprises, uncertainty, turmoil, and violence. Just turn on the television or listen to the radio. We don't have to look far to find trouble. It is on every corner.

At the same time this book is being written, there are social and economic crises in Spain and Greece. The president of the United States and Congress are at a stalemate with the fiscal cliff looming. American Airlines just filed for bankruptcy causing several thousand people to lose their jobs. The teacher's union is on strike in Chicago. War is still raging in Afghanistan and in many other countries; revolutions are erupting everywhere. Health care issues are being debated at the federal and state level. There is a rumor of war in the Middle East. The U.S. ambassador was killed in a riot in Libya. Sex slavery and sex trafficking are on the rise. Bombs exploded at the Boston marathon. There is so much disease and sickness, cancer, social issues, and broken family structures. Prisons are full. People are losing their homes.

One fact that we know about the "storms of life" is that it's no respecter of persons. Gender, race, or financial status makes no difference. It is inevitable. It is not a matter of "if," it is a matter of "when" the storm will come. The storms of life come in different forms and locations, just like natural storms. Florida and a few other states along the East Coast have hurricane to worry about. People who live in the northern states of the U.S. have snow and ice storms to deal with. The West Coast has earthquakes. My family and I live in the state of Oklahoma where we have frequent storms with tornadoes.

To prepare for the storms, many people in Oklahoma have installed storms shelters. My friend David W. Jones owns a storm shelter business. In 2012 his company made 1,056 storm shelter vaults that are built like a bank vault.

David said, "Jesus is the best storm shelter of life. And the best time to prepare for the storm is way before it comes." I have a storm shelter made from concrete with a steel reinforced bunker. Knowing that my family might possibly face a tornado, I had it built when we had our house constructed. However, there are many people who are not prepared for such storms. They are at risk.

Just as we take time and effort to prepare for a tornado, we can also take time to prepare for the storms of life. Jesus said, "You will have suffering in this world." Trouble is coming, and we had better be prepared. Listen to His warning:

> Therefore whosoever heareth these sayings of mine, and doeth them, I will liken him unto a wise man, which built his house upon a rock: And the rain descended, and the floods came, and the winds blew, and beat upon that house; and it fell not: for it was founded upon a rock. And every one that heareth these sayings of mine, and doeth them not, shall be likened unto a foolish man, which built his house upon the sand: And the rain descended, and the floods came, and the winds blew, and beat upon that house; and it fell: and great was the fall of it. —Matthew 7:24–27

In this story, both men heard the instructions. One man chose to follow and one chose to ignore. One man built his house upon the rock. He took the hard way and the right and sure way, which is the way of the Lord. The other man built his house upon sand. He took the easy pathway, the way of man. Both men built their houses, but on different foundations of belief. We know that it is very hard to excavate a foundation in a rock. But it is very easy to dig a foundation in sand. It is more difficult to live a life honoring God than to live a self-serving one. It is easier to live according to the world than to follow after God's way. As you see in this story, both men faced the storms of life, but only one man's house stood firm.

What Jesus is teaching here is extremely profound. There is a right way to prepare for the storms of life. Build your life on the firm foundation. And the strongest foundation is God. The most important thing in life is to have a relationship with God. The second most important is to have great relationship with others. When the storms of life knock at the door, it may be too late. Listen to what Jesus has to say regarding being prepared for the ultimate life.

> Enter ye in at the strait gate: for wide is the gate, and broad is the way, that leadeth to destruction, and many there be which go in thereat. —Matthew 7:13

Some people say that the way of the world is "fun." Anything goes. Sex, drugs, gambling, any kind of obscene movie or music . . . you name it. There are no limitations—only freedom and imagination. Anything goes for pleasure, seduction, and violence. There is very little accountability.

"I can go anywhere and do anything I please," they say. "But the way of God is boring and narrow minded. Worshipping God, reading the Bible and praying, participating in a Bible study group, going on a mission trip, giving your money as tithes and offerings. Study? What? This is not fun at all!"

Some people complain, "This is just too hard!"

Be ready! You never know when the storms of life are going to hit you. Recently, I met a man whose family was hit by the storms of life at the least expected time.

I was at a dental seminar in Oklahoma City. I had stepped outside for a few minutes to get a breath of fresh air when a dental supply sales representative who I know slightly told me a tragic story about his twenty-one-year-old son who was such a good young man. He was in college and met a girl there. He went home with her to meet her mother and was introduced to the drug methadone. He tried it and was found dead the following morning. This man spoke to me with much pain in his heart.

Then he asked me this question, "My boy was so good. Why did God allow such a thing to happen him? He had such potential and such a great future. Why, Dr. Lim?"

My heart broke for his loss. I expressed my sympathy to this gentleman, and told him that I didn't have all the answers, but one thing I do know: God loves us and He is not willing that anyone should perish. His son's death did not happen without God's permission. God knows and understands about his loss. Death, pain, and suffering are part of life. God did not cause it, but He does allow it to happen to fulfill His purpose. God takes the good, the bad, the past, the present, the future, pain, laughter, sorrow, sickness, and health, and He adds all of them up and causes them all to "work together for good to them . . . who are the called according to his purpose" (Romans 8:28)

God's purpose is very definite. The real question to ask, then, is, *What is God's ultimate purpose for man?* People have different answers according to their understanding, but according to the Bible, God's eternal purpose for man is for people to have life and to have it to the fullest. God wants us to experience the ultimate life. And this life can only be found in Him.

Jesus said, "The thief cometh not, but for to steal, and to kill, and to destroy: I am come that they might have life, and that they might have it more abundantly" (John 10:10).

The ultimate life is not found in prosperity, but only in Christ. Last Thanksgiving my family got together. We had three hickory smoked turkeys, chicken and beef curry, mashed potatoes, gravy, and all kinds of pies, ice cream, and special drinks, plus much more. We ate more than we needed, and there was much left over to last a few more meals. Then a few hours later, we ate some more. We had food in abundance. When God talks about His purpose to give us life in abundance, He doesn't mean about our physical appetite. He is really talking about the fulfillment of the heart that nothing else can satisfy except Him.

The Old Testament book of Ecclesiastes says, "He hath made every thing beautiful in his time: also he hath set the world in their heart, so that no man can find out the work that God maketh from the beginning to the end" (Ecclesiastes 3:11).

God created us so intimately special that He made a unique place in our heart that nothing else besides Him can fill. No riches, prosperity, status, or fame can take His place. It's not that God doesn't desire for us to have prosperity and success and fun. He does. But none of that gives long-lasting fulfillment. I thought I had found the ultimate life when I first came to America. I thought my dream had come true, and that nothing else could top it. As good as it was, nothing could compare to the ultimate life I now have in Christ. He gives me eternal fulfillment. I believe that God wants us to be successful and prosperous, but He wants, first and foremost, to have relationship with us. Relationship first lasts.

Jesus said, "But seek ye first the kingdom of God, and his righteousness; and all these things shall be added unto you" (Matthew 6:33).

Throughout the Bible, the Scripture reveals God's eternal intention for man. God's ultimate purpose for you is to have a relationship with Him. The question is, Why? Does God need us? No, He does not need us. The reason is because of His love for us. He made us in the likeness of Himself. He had a relationship with man in the Garden of Eden before sin came into man's heart. Man disobeyed God, and turned away from Him. But God, through His eternal love, sent His Son, Jesus Christ, to pursue us. Listen to this story and you will know how much God really loves us.

> And he said, A certain man had two sons: And the younger of them said to his father, Father, give me the portion of goods that falleth to me. And he divided unto them his living. And not many days after the younger son gathered all together, and took his journey into a far country, and there wasted his substance with riotous living. And when he had spent all, there arose a mighty famine in that land; and he began to be in want. And he went and joined himself to a citizen of that country; and he sent him into his fields to feed swine. And he would fain have filled his belly with the husks that

the swine did eat: and no man gave unto him. And when he came to himself, he said, How many hired servants of my father's have bread enough and to spare, and I perish with hunger! I will arise and go to my father, and will say unto him, Father, I have sinned against heaven, and before thee, And am no more worthy to be called thy son: make me as one of thy hired servants. And he arose, and came to his father. But when he was yet a great way off, his father saw him, and had compassion, and ran, and fell on his neck, and kissed him. And the son said unto him, Father, I have sinned against heaven, and in thy sight, and am no more worthy to be called thy son. But the father said to his servants, Bring forth the best robe, and put it on him; and put a ring on his hand, and shoes on his feet: And bring hither the fatted calf, and kill it; and let us eat, and be merry: For this my son was dead, and is alive again; he was lost, and is found. And they began to be merry.

—Luke 15:11–24

There are many principles we can draw from this story, but the main one is this: God loves us and He desires to have a relationship with us. He is waiting with open arms. The most wonderful thing about our heavenly Father is that He is a gracious and kind God who is waiting for us to return home. It does not matter how far we have gone, what country we have been in, what sins we have committed. The Bible says, "If we confess our sins, he is faithful and just to forgive us our sins, and to cleanse us from all unrighteousness" (1 John 1:9).

Mistakes teach us a lot. Yes, they cost us much pain, but pain is a great teacher. There is a saying, "Necessity is the mother of invention, but pain is the father of teaching." The young son in Jesus' story learns so much from his mistake. He learns that satisfaction in life can only be found in his father's home. He travels far to search for fulfillment only to discover that he had the best at home. He spent all his money to buy things to make him happy. But his happiness was fleeting. There are a lot of people who are rich in this world. They have money to buy a house, but they can't buy a home. They have money to buy a bed, but they can't buy sleep. They don't live their life to fulfill the purpose that God has for them.

No one really knows what the father or the son in this story really looked like. Rembrandt, the world-famous artist, attempted to put flesh on this story with his painting titled "The Return of the Prodigal Son." In his famous painting, the artist beautifully and skillfully portrays the compassionate, loving father standing with both of his hands touching over the shoulders of his son kneeling in front of him. The father looks very noble and royal wearing a rich, warm robe. His head is covered with thick, long hair. In contrast to the nobleness of his father, the young son kneels on the ground projecting poverty with his bare feet exposing callused soles. His body is covered with a thin, pale, and worn out rag. His scalp shows some bald spots with patchy hair. He looks malnourished and grubby. Despite the filth, the father embraces his son with joy and compassion.

In the same painting, Rembrandt painted the older brother wearing rich clothes like the father, but he stands with his arms crossed looking at his poor and broken brother. The older brother's posture looks stiff, unmoving, and distant. He does not show any support to his brother. His body language expresses resentment, bitterness, and jealousy. Sometimes our nonverbal communication speaks louder than words.

I grew up with three brothers, and our mother always told us that she loved each one of us equally, but I knew that was not true. One day in front of all my brothers I asked her, "Mom, who is your favorite son?"

"Heng, I love each one of you the same!" she replied as always.

"Mom, I don't believe you. I think I am your favorite," I teased.

"Son, it is true that I love each one of you the same, but when one of you needs me the most, then that one is my favorite," my mother explained.

In Jesus' story, the youngest son was the father's favorite and that made his oldest brother very angry, prompting him to say this to his father:

> . . . Lo, these many years do I serve thee, neither transgressed I at any time thy commandment: and yet thou never gavest me a kid, that I might make merry with my friends: But as soon as this thy son was come, which hath devoured thy living with harlots, thou hast killed for him the fatted calf. —Luke 15:29–30

Obviously this older brother got his thinking messed up. He thought that his position as a son depended on what he could do for his father, rather than because of who he was. I am so thankful that God does not judge me based on what I can do to get into Heaven. And I am also glad that my older brother, Cheang, was a source of encouragement and support to me while we were growing up together. Cheang always tried to look after me.

When Cheang left to go to college at Southwest Baptist University, he gave me his job. Shortly thereafter, Dortha Harvey moved me upstairs to the recording department. I loved it! My job was to duplicate broadcasting tapes, package them, and mail them to radio stations all over America. I duplicated thousands of cassette tapes for radio show listeners. Part of my daily job requirement was to inspect each tape for sound quality. Every day I listened to thousands of tapes, and each one started with the same introduction. Dr. David Webber with his flowing, manly, baritone voice, speaking each word clearly: "Radio friends, God is still on the throne, and prayer changes things."

In my four years during college while I was working at Southwest Radio Church, I must have heard this truth over a million times. At first I did not pay much attention to it. It must have been at least a few thousand times after I heard it before I really comprehended its full truth. Now everywhere I went, the truth resonated in my mind, my heart, and my total being. At first I thought it was just a catchy phrase, but then I realized that it was the truth.

"God is still on the throne, and prayer changes things." Dr. Noah W. Hutchings, who is now the ninety-one–year–old president of Southwest Radio Church, continues to echo this truth on the broadcast worldwide. He proclaims this truth into the prisons, into third world countries, and far beyond.

Some people don't think about God when things are going well. They hear about God, but they don't want to have anything to do with Him. The mundaneness of life causes them to focus on themselves. They wait until things go wrong, then they seek Him. Such was the case of the young son you just read about.

The prophet of God, Isaiah, penned this truth, "In the year that king Uzziah died I saw also the Lord sitting upon a throne, high and lifted up, and his train filled the temple" (Isaiah 6:1). This vision changed Isaiah's life and gave him a great purpose and passion to serve God. "Also I heard the voice of the Lord, saying, Whom shall I send, and who will go for us? Then said I, Here am I; send me" (Isaiah 6:8). It took the death of a king for the prophet to see the Lord.

I don't know what problems you are facing today. It could be health issues, family, divorce, finances, school, relationships, addiction, pornography, anger, unemployment, jealousy, children, marriage, or anything. Whatever storm of life you are facing today, you can rise above it. The Lord is the one who will fight the battle for you. The Bible says, "No weapon that is formed against thee shall prosper; and every tongue that shall rise against thee in judgment thou shall condemn. This is the heritage of the servants of the LORD, and their righteousness is of me, saith the LORD" (Isaiah 54:17).

Listen to the promise of God through His words. "Do not err, my beloved brethren. Every good gift and every perfect gift is from above, and cometh down from the Father of lights, with whom is no variableness, neither shadow of turning" (James 1:16–17).

God gives good and perfect gifts to His children, but we have to receive them. "I am the door: by me if any man enter in, he shall be saved, and shall go in and out, and find pasture" (John 10:9). He is the door of opportunity and His door swings on the hinges of adversity.

As a young college student, I could not see far ahead into the future that God has promised. Nevertheless I chose to put my trust in Him. Sometimes I had doubt that I was going to make it. I was going to college full time and at the same time working full time. Things were tough. Many times I didn't know if we were going to be able to make ends meet. But the Lord always came through for me. He never failed me.

God can choose to stop the storm, and He can choose to divert the storm—but He always chooses to be with us in the storm. It is the process of going though the storm that strengthens us. Storms of life shape our character. They help define who we are. They take us through a process of transformation. They build our faith and the faith of those around us.

The Lord compares believers to the eagle who can rise above the storm. When storms come, instead of seeking shelter below, the eagle flies high above the storms and rests its wing. In the same way, we can rest in the Lord.

> Hast thou not known? hast thou not heard, that the everlasting God, the LORD, the Creator of the ends of the earth, fainteth not, neither is weary? there is no searching of his understanding. He giveth power to the faint; and to them that have no might he increaseth strength. Even the youths shall faint and be weary, and the young men shall utterly fall: But they that wait upon the LORD shall renew their strength; they shall mount up with wings as eagles; they shall run, and not be weary; and they shall walk, and not faint.
>
> —Isaiah 40:28–31

Chapter 17

Things Have Changed

Quite often when people find out that I am a dentist they react in one of three ways. The first reaction is that the person winces. Second, the person makes that "hilarious" joke about a dentist putting a knee on the chest while pulling a tooth. And third, an older person may ask me, "Does your office still have that belt-driven drill?" Inside, I want to burst out laughing at such remarks, but I normally remain calm and politely respond, "Things have changed, especially in dentistry. Dentists don't just drill, fill, and send patients the bill anymore. We are doing things that change lives."

Here is one example of how far dentistry has changed. Dr. Edie Long, a professor from Northeastern University in Tahlequah, Oklahoma, says about how the new change of dentistry has changed her life. "I had a great deal of pain in my head and neck, as well as throughout my entire body. I was unable to walk even fifty feet without pain in my legs and feet. Now I walk for blocks without pain. I had no idea that teeth and their occlusion were so important. Dr. Lim, you were also able to save and restore my teeth which had broken and cracked from all the years of clenching and grinding. Now I have a healthy beautiful smile and a true reason to smile, because I am pain free. I will ever be grateful to you and your dental team. You are very special to me."

As much as Dr. Long's life has been changed because of what

modern science can do for her, there is one definite change that can radically change people's lives. This change is so extravagant and critical that I would like to share it with you. You see, change creates both problems and opportunities. It causes people to either take action or to fall behind. Sometimes people can see the benefits of the change, but they don't want to go through the process. The process can be painful and difficult. Everything changes. Change is eminent. If we don't keep up, we get left behind.

Another great example of this is the change in new technology. In 1994, when I first got out of dental school, the Motorola cell phone had just become available. It was the size of a brick. After that, things moved rapidly to Razr phones, Bluetooth phones, and iPhones. Add to that iPads, iPods, and much more. I just recently got my first iPhone, and there are now even more new changes.

At our last Thanksgiving dinner, my younger brother, Meng, looked at my cell phone and laughed. I was still using an old flip phone, covered with scratches.

"Brother, you must keep up with the changes, or you will get left behind." He laughed and took the antiquated phone out of my hand. "What is this?" he joked with me.

"Meng, my phone works just fine." I tried to defend myself in front of my mother and the other family members.

"Son, Meng is right. You better change and keep up. You'll be left behind." My mother tag-teamed with my younger brother in their assault.

I told my mother that she was right and that I was trying my best to keep up. I told her that I just bought a CAD–CAM (Computer Aided Design–Computer Aided Manufacturing) six months ago for my dental office. Mark, my friend and the sales rep, said that it was supposed to be the latest and best computer system that technology has to offer. It will help me to make crowns and restorations for teeth and dental implants in just one appointment. I was just informed that there is already a new upgraded version available. Our office also just bought a 3-D cone beam x-ray machine. It works like a CAT scan. I can scan the patient and look at the image from any kind of angle. All of this technology is supposed to be the latest and the best.

Meng told me that if I were staying the night at my mother's house he would bring me his old iPhone 3G to try, and if I liked it, I could keep it. I agreed and accepted his gift the following morning. I can see why people really like new technology. Having the ability to communicate with anyone anywhere in the world and having access to all kinds of information at your fingertips is a BIG change from the Pony Express of the Wild West. New technology has improved our way of living drastically, and changes will continue relentlessly. Like my brother said, if we don't keep up with the changes, we may be left behind.

As critical as technological change is, it doesn't last. There is always something new being developed. However, there is one change that will definitely last. This change is critical. It is the change that will affect people's destiny. It is the ultimate life change. Without this change, people will be left behind for eternity. If people decide to embrace this one change it will be the best, most awesome decision they will ever make. Everything in our world will fade away, but this one change will remain forever. This change is so radical and powerful that it has transformed my life and many others.

"I feel like a million bucks," a fisherman in Montana said about this change.

"My destiny has been changed," one successful businessman in Kauai declared.

"I am no longer a sex slave. I am a princess," a Cambodian girl testified.

What if a king were to graciously offer you the gift of a lifetime? What if he were to invite you to become his son or daughter and heir to his throne? Would you be willing to change your life to accommodate the royal offer? Of course you would. The change I am speaking of is the change for an eternity. It is a spiritual change for a sinner to become a child of God. A change from hopeless to hopeful; from a sad life to a joyful life; from being the enemy of God to being a friend of God; from being fearful to peaceful; from being a nobody to a somebody; from being chained to being free; from being a sinner to being a saint; from being a slave to being a prince or princess.

God is the agent of this change. He is the King of Kings. He sent Jesus Christ His Son to earth. He died on the cross in our place for our sins. The Bible calls this death a vicarious death. He was buried in the grave for three days. Then He arose from the dead. He conquered death. After revealing Himself, and before going back up to Heaven, He commissioned His disciples to go into the entire world to proclaim the message of the ultimate life, the message that God loves us, He has forgiven our sin, and He is not willing that anyone should perish. To all who receive Him, He gave the right to become children of God to those who believe in His Name.

This is the best news and the best deal ever! What an unfair exchange for God—His Son in exchange for no-good sinners such as you and me. We received the better deal by becoming children of God. It cost God everything, but it cost us nothing. The Bible says, "For he hath made him to be sin for us, who knew no sin; that we might be made the righteousness of God in him" (2 Corinthians 5:21).

This is His grace: God's riches at Christ's expense. Jesus explains His grace like this, ". . . I am come that they might have life, and that they might have it more abundantly" (John 10:10).

The Bible teaches us that a person goes through this spiritual change by accepting Jesus Christ as his personal substitute for the penalty of sin. Once he becomes a child of God, God begins a process in him that changes the sinner to become like Christ in his attitude, ambition, actions, thoughts, speech, and conduct. God uses many things to accomplish His purpose, including His Spirit, His Word, His church, trials and circumstances, and Christian friends.

The spiritual change to the ultimate life is not something that happens all at once. It is a process. This process is called "growth."

This growth happens from the inside. It is a change from within us, not all around us. We know that we live in a radical and fast-changing world. Nothing around us stays the same. Things change, and so do people. We live in a world of uncertainty, with chaos and many problems, most of which are beyond our control. We may not be able to control our surroundings, but we can control what is within us. We cannot be responsible for the behavior of others, but we are totally, one hundred percent responsible for our own behavior. Our greatest problems are never around us—they are within us.

Regarding the problems we face, Jesus puts it simply, "For from within, out the heart of men, proceed evil thoughts, adulteries, fornications, murders, Thefts, covetousness, wickedness, deceit, lasciviousness, an evil eye, blasphemy, pride, foolishness: All these evil things come from within, and defile the man" (Mark 7:21–23).

There are many Christians who are not living their lives victoriously, as God has intended for them. One reason is that they don't take full responsibility for their problems. They blame their problems on others. But Theodore Roosevelt said, "If you could kick the person in the pants responsible for most of your trouble, you wouldn't sit for a month."

Eleanor Roosevelt said it like this: "No one can make you feel inferior without your consent." Since the fall of Adam, man has continually attempted to shift the blame onto someone else.

On a lighter note, I am reminded of a story of a pastor who was visiting a member of his church. While he was knocking on the door of the house, he noticed a light was on inside, and he saw the shadow of a person scurrying around, trying to hide behind the curtain in the front window. It was obvious that someone was inside the house, so he continued to knock, but to no avail. At last he took out his church business card and wrote Revelation 3:20 on the back: "Behold, I stand at the door, and knock: if any man hear my voice, and open the door, I will come in to him, and will sup with him, and he with me," and signed his name. The following Sunday, the same card was found in the offering plate. The lady of the house returned it with the scripture from Genesis 3:10, ". . . I heard thy voice in the garden, and I was afraid, because I was naked; and I hid myself."

We cannot shift blame and ungodly behavior onto someone else when we are under pressure. God's Word is clear. We don't sin due to social, medical, financial, or environmental pressure. We sin because of our sinful heart. In my youth, my Sunday school teacher at Northwest Baptist Church, Norman Cantrell, would not let me give him an excuse for any of my failures. He used to tell me, "Heng, excuses are lies wrapped in the package of reasons."

My family enjoys drinking hot jasmine tea, especially in the winter. It gives us a warm feeling inside. Normally, to make tea, we place the tea bag in the tea pot of boiled water for a few minutes. The hot water does not have a taste, but the water reveals the flavor of the tea in the bag. The human heart is similar. The hot water experience we go through does not produce bitterness, anger, jealousy, and depression. It merely reveals who we are.

Several of us know that there are areas of our lives that we need to change. We are not pleased with what we see in ourselves, so we set out to make a change. We try really hard, but we fail over and over again. We want to be like Christ, but we don't really know how to do so. As Christians we are changed as we cooperate with God's leadership. Being led by God's spirit is the evidence of our salvation.

The same instruction God gave people in the past also applies to us today. God's wisdom never changes. It is timeless. His wisdom crosses generations, time, and cultures. You have the choice to choose life and prosperity, or death and adversity. Most people would choose life and prosperity, as did the queen of England.

When Queen Victoria was a teenager in school, she did not choose to apply herself. She thought school was boring. Nor she did understand the purpose for studying. Her teachers tried to encourage her to study diligently, but she didn't want to put forth the effort, until one day her teacher let her in on a secret. The secret was that she was next in line to the throne of England. Realizing her destiny, she began to change and apply herself, because she wanted to be a good queen.

Likewise, our heavenly Father is the King of Kings. He rules the universe. Believers are His children and heirs of the King, destined to be great. We must change and apply ourselves while we have the opportunity. Today it seems that many people have an entitlement mentality. They want the result, but they are not willing to put forth the effort. People want the results now and they want to pay later. Listen to what our heavenly Father said, "I the LORD search the heart, I try the reins, even to give every man according to his ways, and according to the fruit of his doings" (Jeremiah 17:10).

God is a loving Father. He wants what is best for each one of us. The question is, If God gives you the opportunity to change, will you seize it?

Chapter 18

God Is Big Enough to Rule the Universe, But . . .

Rachel my wife usually drives our daughter to school, but once in a while I get the privilege. Rebekah attends Claremore Christian Academy, a small private school located about nine miles from our home. To get to her school, we drive on beautiful scenic Highway 88, crossing Lake Oologah Dam. Most of the time in the morning a family of doe and fawns are grazing along the road at the edge of the wood. The view is very peaceful. Sometimes people are too busy looking at the beautiful scenery to pay attention to the curvy road. That can be deadly dangerous. Drivers normally don't slow down, and as a result many major accidents have occurred there. The latest one was a semi truck that was going too fast, lost control, and turned over, spilling its chemical cargo and killing the driver.

Sometimes I find myself in a hurry to get to my future, and I am totally oblivious to my loved ones. As I crossed the dam seeing the tragic accident, it reminded me of how fragile life really is. I realized that life is but a vapor. It does not seem that long ago that I drove my wife across this dam to the hospital for the birth of Rebekah. And now Rebekah is fifteen years old.

One day on the way to her school, Rebekah and I had an interesting and meaningful conversation. I opened up the conversation by asking Rebekah, "What do you think 'faith' is?" I caught her by surprise. It was still so early in the morning, and her attention was on her science project in the back seat of the truck.

Her response was something like this. "Uh, faith? Dad?" She had a puzzled look on her face as she looked at me from the back seat.

"Yes, faith, baby. What do people think of faith?" For a moment, I thought she was going to say, "Faith moved out of her parents' house." But Rebekah spoke softly, saying, "Faith? Dad, many people say that seeing is believing."

"Go on," I urged.

"But I have to say, there are a lot of microbes that cause us to get sick. We can't see them with our naked eye. Then, there is the air that we breathe that we can't see, and many other things we can't see with our eyes, but they do exist. Faith, then, is seeing something with your heart that you cannot see with your eyes," Rebekah reasoned wisely. "If we believe in something that we can actually see, then it is not really faith-based," she added.

I interjected that there are a lot of people who do not believe God exists because they can't see Him. She agreed with that. I then proceeded to ask Rebekah what she believed to be true.

"Dad, do you see the wind?" she asked. "We can't see the wind blow, but you can see the evidence. It is the same with God. No one has seen a visual of God, especially in these days, but we can see His evidence everywhere."

"What about deism? What do you make of it?" I asked Rebekah. She looked puzzled once more, unaware of what I was asking.

"The deist believes that God is the Creator of the universe, but after He finished creating, He took himself out of the picture and now sits on the throne somewhere, not intervening or getting involved with His creation." I asked Rebekah if this is what she believed. She assured me that she did not.

"Dad?" she proceeded to ask. "Do you remember one mission trip when our family took a group of college students to Cambodia?"

She switched the direction I was going with this, but I played along with her and answered that I remembered. "One student told me that I can be a Christian and I don't have to change a thing," she explained. "He said that I can be a Christian and live the same way as I did before. I can live like the world." I was quite aware of who the young man was that Rebekah was talking about. I questioned my daughter by asking her, "What is your take on that, Rebekah, concerning being a follower of Jesus Christ and not having to change a thing?" She answered, "Well the Scripture says we have to be born again, Dad."

"That is right, baby. We do. The Scripture says that, 'Therefore, if any man be in Christ, he is a new creature: old things are passed away; behold, all things are become new'" (2 Corinthians 5:17).

I added, "Another scripture says clearly that we must not remain the same as before. 'I beseech you, therefore, brethren, by the mercies of God, that ye present your bodies a living sacrifice, holy, acceptable unto God, which is your reasonable service" (Romans 12:1).

I looked at her quickly and asked, "Whose responsibility is it to present ourselves as a living sacrifice?" Then I turned my attention back on the road.

"We the believers are responsible!" she reasoned.

"Do we have to change to become more godly?" I added

"We sure do," she responded.

"Listen to this verse from the Bible." I quoted, "And be not conformed to this world: but be ye transformed by the renewing of your mind, that ye may prove what is that good, and acceptable, and perfect, will of God" (Romans 12:2).

Just as we got into the most meaningful part of the discussion, we arrived at our destination, the school parking lot. I parked the truck. She opened the passenger door, and while keeping it wide open she opened the back door and grabbed her insect collection and backpack. Then she shut the back door.

"Goodbye, Dad. I love you!" she said, while closing the front door and walking toward the school building.

As I drove out of the parking lot and made my way to my office, my heart was full of joy and gratitude. I was praising God all the way to work for His blessings upon my life. I was thanking Him for my beautiful wife, my two daughters, my job, but most of all I thanked Him for being such a loving God who has a desire to get involved with our daily life. He is not a God who just created us and leaves us to our own devices. Instead His Spirit works within us to change us and transform us toward godliness. I also thanked Him for the truth that He clearly reveals to my family and me.

What about you? Do you know the truth about God? Do you know that God loves you? Have you heard about His forgiveness and redemption plan? Do you know that God has a plan for your life? Would it surprise you to know that God cares for you deeply and He wants to help you? God wants to be your Saviour. He desires to rescue and save you from your despair, giving you a new life, the ultimate life. You may already know this, or you may not. The Scripture says, "Thus saith the Lord the maker thereof, the Lord that formed it, to establish it; the Lord is his name; Call unto me, and I will answer thee, and shew thee great and mighty things, which thou knowest not" (Jeremiah 33:2–3).

What an incredible truth we find in this scripture. The Lord is the one who made the earth and established it, and we live on His property. Not only does He allow us to live here, but He said to call to Him when we don't have the answers to life, when we lose our way, when we want to know great and wondrous things. He must know that we can get lost in life here on earth and that is why He has extended the invitation.

I have called on God and He has done for me more than I could ever imagine. He has given me the ultimate life. God is not a powerful being who created the universe and then said, "It is good. I am done. Now I can sit in my rocking chair for the next few million years and see what will happen." Our God is an intimate, loving God. He wants to get involved with our lives. He is a loving Father and has a plan for us.

What kind of future and hope can God give us? The best, the most supreme, and I believe, the ultimate future and hope. He can and will change anyone who calls on Him. God can change the worst circumstance to make them the best. He can solve the issues that we cannot. But He requires faith.

In his book *Science of Success,* Dr. Napoleon Hill said, "There is no such reality as passive faith. Action is the first requirement of all faith." When we apply faith to whatever definite purpose that God calls us to, He will give us the means and the ability to finish. The Apostle Paul confirms this, "But my God shall supply all your need according to his riches in glory by Christ Jesus" (Philippians 4:19).

God is at work. And He works through men of faith. Recently I met such a man. His name is Jonathan Dougherty.

Jonathan and his family are believers who resided in Claremore, Oklahoma. They answered the call of the Lord to be missionaries to Mongolia. Since he was a child, Jonathan had an interest in the Mongolian culture. He studied and read everything he could find. Eventually, he married Melodie and they had three children.

Brother Jonathan said, "Regarding missions, I have never told my wife where I wanted to go, what I wanted to do, or how. But she knows about my passion." His wife was in total agreement about going to Mongolia. Putting their dream house up for sale and saying goodbye to their parents and loved ones were two of the biggest challenges in making the decision. Jonathan had his house listed on the market for two and a half years. Finally, they could not wait any longer so they decided to go ahead and leave for the mission field. Putting their faith in action, they believed that God would take care of the sale of the house. They set a date: January 14, 2013.

Brother Jonathan said, "A week before the trip the Lord told me, 'Start moving your stuff out of the house and I will do the rest.'" Jonathan further explained, "I am a very cautious man. I don't make a move until I believe it is the Lord directing me. I just don't act on emotion." So by faith the family started moving their belongings out of the house. The house was in a mess and empty. "My home represents me. As a man, I have always attached my identity with my ability and what I have in my home. Sitting there in an empty home, I was on an emotional roller coaster." Jonathan prayed, "My identity is with you now, Jesus. Do with me whatever you please."

"God showed up when I started to move," Jonathan said. "The city manager of Claremore called me informing me that there was a gentleman who wanted to take a look at my house that day. The gentleman is a businessman from Korea. He came and looked at my messy, undecorated house. He offered me exactly the price I asked for, not a penny less and not a penny more. The contract is signed and my house is sold," Jonathan bragged on God. "I put the house up for sale. For two and half years we kept it meticulously clean, spotless, and decorated. We showed it only two times. Then as soon as I started moving the stuff out like the Lord instructed me to do, I had nine calls in two days."

I have known Jonathan and his family for a long time. His parents are great people. We all agree that he is a very godly man. He loves to hunt. Now, instead of hunting bear and elk, he is hunting men for Jesus. I asked him, "What can you learn from this?" He said, "Faith without action is dead. God is ready for us to make a move so that He can show up." After Jonathan finished moving his belongings out of his house, he brought his trailer to me. "I can never repay you for what you have done for my family. I want to give you my trailer," Jonathan told me.

When you hear a story like this, you've got to believe and trust in God, that He is real and He is with us right here and right now. Many people have asked this question: "How do you know that God is real?" The answer is that we know Him by faith. The Bible says, "Now faith is the substance of things hoped for, the evidence of things not seen" (Hebrews 11:1). Faith allows us to see God with the eyes of our heart. Faith in God also gives us hope in spite of the circumstances and points us in another direction.

Here is a great story of another man that demonstrates faith. Paul works at the men's suit department at Dillard's in Woodland Hills Mall in Tulsa, Oklahoma. From the moment my wife and I walked into that department, we noticed there was something different about Paul's attitude toward us. Paul was dressed in a pair of nice dress pants and a white dress shirt and tie, with shiny black shoes. He walked with a limp, dragging his right leg. I observed that the man must have been partially paralyzed on the right side. He appeared to be in his forties. As soon as he saw us walking into his department, he walked right up to us, welcoming us with a friendly smile.

"How may I help you?" he asked. When I inquired as to the whereabouts of a restroom he directed us there.

Paul had noticed, with a compassionate expression on his face, that my wife was walking with the assistance of a walker due to a recent knee surgery. Paul proceeded to insist that we follow him in the direction of the restroom. He and my wife chatted for a little while about their common disabilities. Here was a man willing to assist us when, in reality, he could probably sit at home feeling sorry for himself and collecting disability, but instead had chosen to make a living for himself. There was something definitely different about this man. Once we saw the sign for the restroom, we insisted he stay and we proceeded to the facility on our own.

We later returned to the men's department and purchased a few pairs of pants. "Heng," Paul said, "your alterations will be ready to pick up next Monday." With that statement, he put the receipts together with his left hand, grasped the stapler with his withered right hand and stapled them together.

While looking at his skinny right hand, I asked Paul what had happened to him. With a big grin on his face, he replied, "Oh, don't feel sorry for me. It was the best thing that ever happened to me. Do you know Darin Spoo? He is my pastor at First Baptist Church of Tulsa," he explained.

I replied that I had not had the privilege of meeting him yet. Paul explained that he and his family were members at this church and were very happy there. I could sense that he was a very devoted church member, but he still was not giving me the information that I was looking for regarding his unfortunate circumstance. "Paul," I once again asked, "what happened to you?"

Here's the story Paul shared with me.

Paul was nineteen years old, a student at Oklahoma State University, and heading out to get into all kinds of foolishness. He and his fraternity brothers were on their way to a Dallas football game, driving 135 miles per hour on I-35 South when they hydroplaned and hit a bridge. The left side of his head hit the concrete so hard that it constricted the left side of the brain. He was in a coma for two and a half months. He smiled as he told his story, and then pulled a handkerchief from his pocket to wipe the sweat from his brow. He testified, "It was the best thing that ever happened to me." I was astonished at this statement. So I stopped him and asked, "What do you mean? This accident that put you in a coma for two and half months and left you almost crippled was the best thing for you?"

Paul smiled and declared his faith, "I don't know where I would be if God had not intervened in my life." Taking his iPhone from his pocket, he showed me and Rachel a picture. "Look here. I have a beautiful daughter. My wife, daughter, and I are so happy. Don't feel sorry for me. God has changed my life."

As my wife and I left the mall that day, Paul's words continued to echo in my mind, "It was the best thing that ever happened to me! I don't know where I would be if God had not intervened in my life!" Paul had found true happiness, or true happiness had found Paul. Paul has faith to see that God is big enough to rule the universe, but small enough to live in his heart. Paul's life reminds me of what Jesus said, "He that findeth his life shall lose it: and he that loseth his life for my sake shall find it" (Matthew 10:39).

Paul demonstrated that life apart from trusting in Jesus is meaningless. God is the true source of happiness. Anything else is but an imitation of joy. The true answer in life is not found in the party scene, education, accomplishments, or popularity, but only in God. Paul has found true happiness, which was spoken of by the prophet Jeremiah. "Blessed [or how very happy] is the man that trusteth in the LORD, and whose hope the LORD is. For he shall be as a tree planted by the waters, and that spreadeth out her roots by the river, and shall not see when heat cometh, but her leaf shall be green; and shall not be careful in the year of drought, neither shall cease from yielding fruit" (Jeremiah 17:7–8).

So you see, God is still changing lives for those who believe Him. He desires to be a part of the life of any person who is willing to trust Him. The Bible says, "Come unto me, all ye that labour and are heavy laden, and I will give you rest" (Matthew 11:28).

Knowing that God is the answer to the ultimate life, I will give my life to honor Him and to tell other people about His glory.

Chapter 19

In God We Trust

"Doctor, you have a phone call," my assistant informed me behind her surgical mask. "Thank you, Misty," I politely replied, while glancing over my shoulder at the blinking communications panel on the wall in the operatory. I'm thinking to myself that this must be an important call. Joyce, my trusted dental concierge, knows that I only take phone calls from three people during certain dental procedures—my wife, another professional, and my pastor. I excused myself from the operatory, removing my mask and gloves, and I walked to the hallway phone. Picking up the receiver, I said, "Hello, this is Dr. Lim. How may I help you?"

"Hello, Heng, this is Mel," replied the voice on the other end of the phone.

"Hello, Mel." I was puzzled as to the nature of this emergency.

"Congratulations, Heng!" Mel continued. "You are the proud owner of two, healthy newborn calves!" Mel had taken my two very pregnant cows to his barn so that he could keep an eye on them.

I was so excited to hear about the birth of my first two calves that I shouted out the news to all who could hear in the office, disturbing the normal dental office protocol. As I regained my composure, I went back to the phone conversation with Mel.

"What is your branding letter, Heng? What letter or symbol do you want to use on your cows and calves?" Mel asked. I have seen those brandings he is talking about, such as "Flying J." I was in deep thought as to what I should choose for a branding name. I wanted it to be something special.

It was about then that Mel exclaimed with a suggestion, "I've got one for you, Heng, Triple C," Mel laughed.

Triple C? I thought, my name doesn't even have a 'C' in it. "What does that stand for, Mel?" I asked.

I was surprised with the answer Mel gave me, "Crazy Cambodian Cowboy," Mel laughed heartily, at my expense of course.

I liked Triple C, but I had another meaning for it. "Christian Cambodian Cowboy," I informed Mel. I want it to remind me of where I came from. I may be the first "Cambodian redneck" in Oklahoma, but that is okay. I want people to know the reason we are blessed to be here in Oologah, Oklahoma, is because of what Christ has done for us. I want everyone to wonder as they drive past our ranch and see our cattle and horses how a family from Cambodia ended up in Oologah, Oklahoma.

Mel is a friend. As a matter of fact, he is my neighbor. My staff often joke around with me regarding my "neighbors." It seems that anyone living within a ten-mile radius from me in Oologah, Oklahoma, is considered my neighbor. I must confess I do have many wonderful neighbors.

"Oologah" is an Indian word, meaning "dark cloud." It does live up to its name. Coming into town, people can see dark smoke perpetually rising out of the huge three-hundred-foot smokestack of the local power plant. At night this power plant, all lit up, looks like a cruise ship. In the morning, older gentlemen sit in the Daylight Donut shop visiting. Oologah is a beautiful, charming town. It's the birthplace of the cowboy Will Rogers. As a matter of fact, his old house, the Dog Iron Ranch, is still standing over by Lake Oologah. Will Rogers is "the famous son of Oklahoma," the "cowboy of all cowboys." Will is famous for many quotes, but the most famous one is, "I never met a man I didn't like."

Entering into Oologah are train tracks running parallel with Highway 169. You definitely know when the train is coming or going due to the shrill sound of the horn blasting at any given time, day or night. Mel and Peggy Dainty live a few hundred feet east of the train tracks, a few miles northeast of my house. They are incredible people. Mel is definitely a cowboy, and Peggy is a true city woman!

Lake Oologah is only a few miles away from my home. People from all over Oklahoma come to camp there. My family and I have camped there several times. It is a great place for water ski-ing and fishing. It is beautiful there around spring and early summer. Dogwood and redbuds bloom colorfully. There is a nice hiking trail over the bluff overlooking the lake, and a picnic table for the family. But Oologah can get very hot and humid during late July and August. Instead of staying here when it is very hot, our family would rather go vacationing in the north where it is cooler.

On our twenty-second anniversary, Rachel and I spent ten days in Livingston, Montana. We went there with our friends, Harry and Ginger Creech, and our daughter, Rebekah. We stayed in a beautiful log cabin in the mountains. While there, Harry hired a professional fishing guide to escort us down the Yellowstone River. Our desire was to do some trout fishing. This place was known as the "fly-fishing capital of the world." Several months before the trip, Harry and I had spent a great deal of time practicing our fishing techniques. We went to the Bass Pro Shop in Broken Arrow and picked up some really nice equipment—rods, reels, vests, boots, waders, lures, lines, hooks, etc. I had personally invested a great deal of time and resources for this trip but, of course, fishing was not our priority—celebrating our anniversary was (or should have been). However, after all the time and resources we spent on fishing gear, it became apparent that fly fishing was our priority.

When we got to our destination in Montana, we met up with our professional fishing guide, "Red Beard." Red Beard told us that he had been a fishing guide for ten years or more and loved his job.

He told us that he had gone to school in Ohio to become a physician, but could not stand the sight of blood. I noticed that both of his palms had calluses the size of grapes. His skin was thick and leathery. He told us that he had packed up everything he owned, put it in his suburban, and moved to Montana. This was more than ten years ago.

He informed us that we were not far from the area where the movie *A River Runs Through It* was filmed. He said that all the women want to stand on the rock where Brad Pitt stood and did his shadow casting. (Shadow casting is a technique of whipping the fly fishing rod back and forth above the head, keeping the fishing line and the fly in the air.) Red Beard also told us that the Gallatin River was not far from there, and that his friend was actually the one who stood in for Brad Pitt on the famous rock in the movie.

Red Beard is a rough, tough, wild outdoorsman who loves to fish and hunt. He guides 182 days out of the year. When Harry and I were fishing, the salmon flies hatched. Salmon flies exist on the bottom of the river as nymphs for seven years. Then at the perfect time, they hatch, fly on the river, and mate. Trout love to eat them. Their wings look more like dragonfly wings, but their abdomens are thick, pale yellow flesh about an inch and a half long. They were everywhere, flying and crawling in our shirts, pants, and boat. I asked Red Beard what they tasted like. He said he didn't know as he reached into the air to grab the insect by the wings between his thumb and finger to examine it. He then twisted the wings.

He said, "I had a plan with this insect." Seeing him playing with the fly, I said, "If trout love to eat them, then they must taste really good and be very healthy for you." I urged Red Beard to take a bite.

"No way!" Red Beard contested. At this time, Harry was sitting in the back of the boat. He reached into the air, grabbed the bug from Red Beard's fingers, peeled the wings off, and quickly stuck it into his mouth and took a bite! It happened so quickly, like a lizard catching a fly with his tongue.

"Hey, Heng, it doesn't taste bad at . . ." Before Harry could even finish his sentence, I reached for a bug in the air. I popped the whole thing into my mouth and crunched away on it.

"Gross! Sick! You guys are gross!" Red Beard moaned. Then he questioned us as to what it tasted like. Harry, being an engineer, was very calculated with his words. He was fishing for the right words to describe this gross, juicy bug in his mouth. Before he could spew out the words, I spoke up.

"It tastes like crickets and butterfly larvae, or maybe raw, freshwater shrimp. Go ahead, eat one, Red Beard. Eat one! I double dare you. You'll never know until you taste one," I insisted.

Red Beard reached into the side of the boat and grasped a thick salmon fly with his fingers. He carefully plucked off the wings and the head, tossed them overboard, and with an excruciating look on his face he popped the bug into his mouth and started chewing. "Not bad! In over ten years, I have never met anyone like you two," he retorted.

"Red Beard, I have eaten worse things than that in Cambodia. You think we are crazy, don't you?" I asked. Red Beard couldn't decide if he should say yes or no. He was trying to be polite and certainly didn't want to hurt our feelings.

"Red Beard, what famous people have you met since you have been a guide?' I asked.

"Quite a few," he replied, "but not anyone like you." He led the boat out to the deep. As I was casting toward the bank, I asked Red Beard if anyone had ever shared with him the greatest news.

"Cast to that spot, Heng. Mend it! Strip! Strip it again!" Red Beard was coaching me how to fish in fishermen terminology. He then turned to me and answered "no," he had never been told the good news. "Cast again toward the bank," Red Beard pointed, as he tried to slow the boat down from flowing too rapidly down the river. With an oar in each hand, Red Beard backstroked against the current up the river. I had missed the spot. The boat flowed down the current too fast. I was busy shadow casting.

"Hey, Brad Pitt! Shadow casting is only good for looks, not for catching trout out here," Red Beard joked with me.

By this time, Harry had already caught several white fish and a few cutthroat trout. On the other hand, I had not landed one fish! Red Beard instructed me to cast into the pocket near the bank. "Mend it, mend it, strip, and strip," he coached me.

Suddenly, a huge trout broke the surface of the water and attacked my fly! "I got one!" I shouted with great joy. I played with the fish for a while by holding the tip of my fishing pole up. Red Beard got a dip net, reached into the water, got the fish out, unhooked the fish, and then we posed for the picture, with Harry as the designated photographer. What great joy and what a great catch! It was a big, beautiful cutthroat trout, native to the Yellowstone River. We released him back into the water.

Jesus must have known the joy of being a fisherman. His first two disciples were fishermen. They were Simon and Andrew, and Jesus called to them, ". . . Come ye after me, and I will make you to become fishers of men" (Mark 1:17).

On that very day, on the Yellowstone River, I had the privilege to experience the joy of being a fly fisherman, and the joy of being a "fisher of men." Right there on the riverbank I had the privilege of leading Red Beard through the experience of salvation in Jesus Christ. Red Beard received the ultimate life. As soon as Red Beard said "Amen" to the sinner's prayer, he raised his hands to the air, turned in a circle and shouted, "I feel like a million bucks!" I had the honor to baptize him underneath the bridge right there in his home river. The Yellowstone River is very cold, so the baptism was quick. As soon as he burst forth out of that cold river, he exclaimed, "I am cleansed!"

There was much joy that day on the bank of the Yellowstone River. We had fun catching trout, but nothing compared to the joy I had in my heart in "catching" Red Beard for the Lord. On that day the angels in Heaven were celebrating because of one lost soul who had found his way home.

I asked Red Beard how many people he had taken down the river in his ten-plus years as a fishing guide. He told me he had guided thousands, but he had never had anyone tell him about the Lord. I reminded him that now not only could he have the opportunity to be a fisherman, but he could also be a "fisher of men." Harry told him that he could hold his own church service on the river. What a day! Harry and I both felt so blessed. We couldn't wait to get back to our cabin and tell our wives about our "catch of the day!"

As we were driving back, I was thinking that there are lost souls everywhere in the world, even here in "fisherman's paradise." I felt blessed to be here at the right time and in the right place to bring the greatest news of Jesus Christ to my new friend, Red Beard. Just before we said goodbye to him, we took some money out of our wallets to give to him for the trip and for being a great fishing guide. On the currency it reads, "In God We Trust," once again reminding me of the people that need to trust God, especially in Cambodia. Now I know why the Lord directed me to go to Montana instead of going to Cambodia on a mission trip. And while I was in Montana, twenty missionaries from my team were in Cambodia as "fishers of men."

Chapter 20

Paradise

O give thanks unto the LORD; call upon his name: make known his
deeds among the people. Sing unto him, sing psalms unto him: talk
ye of all his wondrous works.   —Psalm 105:1–2

Rachel and I had flown to an island. Our flight arrived late at night.
We gathered our belongings from the baggage claim and proceeded
to the car rental. We got our car and started to drive toward our destination. Rachel and I had been looking forward to this time together
for a year, a time for just the two of us to get away. No kids, no
responsibility. I couldn't wait to get to our vacationing place somewhere on the beach, a romantic getaway. But we had to get there first.

As we were driving from the airport, a torrential rainstorm
poured down on us. Sheets of water splattered over the windshield.
I switched the windshield wipers to the fastest speed, but it still did
not give me much visibility. The road was treacherous—wet, twisting
and turning, narrow and dark. There was a concrete barricade, and
orange construction signs littered the road.

"Help me and keep your eyes on the road, darling," I asked my
wife. "It is so dark, I can't see anything. But according to the map, I
am on the right road . . . I think."

"Are you sure?" Rachel second-guessed me.

"No, I am not sure, darling," I responded with my eyes squinting and concentrating on the road.

"Be careful," Rachel warned me. "The road looks very dangerous. Turn on your high beams."

I tell her I already had.

"Turn on the fog light," she added. I did what she said, but it turned the high beam off, so I turned it back off. There in the dark of the night, we felt so lost and alone. No other vehicle was in sight going the same direction. I drove very slowly, trying to keep the car from hydroplaning. Once in a while a vehicle would come speeding toward us, with high beams glaring our vision, splashing sheets of water on our windshield. I sat at the edge of the driver's seat, leaning forward, trying to concentrate on the road. I looked at the clock on the dash of the car. It was late—eleven at night. We should have been at the condo an hour ago.

"Maybe we are on the wrong island," I thought. "No! It cannot be!" To confirm my suspicions, I found a gas station and stopped to ask for directions. Like most men, I don't like doing this unless I really have to. I spotted a little gas station beside the road and, pulling in, I asked a local native man standing next to his pickup truck for directions. He answered me with a smile.

"Aloha. It would be my pleasure to assist you."

"Is this the road to go to Hanalei Bay?" I asked him.

"You are on the right road. Just keep on driving and you will not miss it. This is the only road going up and it is the only one coming down. Hanalei is to your right," he confirmed.

Relieved that I was on the right island, I thanked the gentleman and got back on the road. "We are on the right path. We should be at the condo within the hour," I told Rachel.

I kept on driving for at least another hour. The night got colder and darker. The road got more curvy and constricted and harder to drive. The shadow of a deep cliff appeared to be on the right side of the road, and a mountain on the left. But it was too dark. I couldn't be sure. The road led us down to a gloomy, narrow one-lane wooden bridge in the woods. I had missed the exit. We were really lost. Carefully crossing this "Bridge of Doom," I tried to comfort Rachel by saying, "Go to sleep. When we get there I'll wake you up."

Snapping back at me in a resentful tone of voice she said, "You are living up to the middle letter of your name." I knew what she meant. "L" is for lost. Feeling really irritated at her comment, I kept silent.

"Let's just pull beside the road and sleep here," Rachel sighed.

"The place looks creepy and unsafe. Let me keep on driving, until I see another gas station or a store to ask for directions." Far ahead I saw a dim light. I was relieved. As I drove closer to the light, I saw a building that looked like a small bar beside the road with a big sign that read "Blue Dolphin." I stopped and ran in, asking a man who was cleaning the tables for directions. "You have come too far. You need to turn back, cross the wooden bridge, and keep on driving until you see a little shopping center. Then you will turn left at the huge, ornate gate with lights and a shooting water fountain."

That night Rachel and I were so lost on that island. The man at the Blue Dolphin finally got me on the right path to our condo. Once I followed his instruction, we arrived safely at our destination. Exhausted and worn out, we checked in and went to sleep.

Have you ever felt lost and confused? You don't know where you are going with life? You feel that your life is full of surprises, with twisting and turning paths. At times you may feel alone. Troubles such as debt, sickness, broken relationships, and even death sneak into your path and cause much heartache. What do you do when that happens? Do you consult with God?

God is true to His Word. His Word is our guide. When we follow after His instructions He promises us blessings. You can trust God. He will never send you on the wrong path. He loves and cares for you. He wants to restore you fully. It does not matter what kind of sin you have committed, what kind of life you have lived, or where you have been, God can help and change you. He wants to lavish you with His love. But there is one thing that you must do. You must repent.

Jesus says, "I tell you, Nay: but, except ye repent, ye shall all likewise perish" (Luke 13:3). To repent means to turn away. You turn away from your sin and shame toward God. That night on the island I was lost, driving in the wrong direction in the dark. After the man in the restaurant told me the right path, I changed my direction and started driving toward the right destination.

I followed the man's direction. I got back on the wooden bridge. I drove up the hill, and in less than twenty minutes I found the gigantic, beautiful, ornate gate. Light shined brightly on the gate. I don't know how I could have missed it earlier. I turned in at the gate and found our destination. We checked into our condo and almost immediately fell asleep.

Then came the morning. The dark island, once it was illuminated, transformed into a paradise. We woke up to a beautiful sunrise on the bay of Hanalei. The beach was pristine. The water was a deep emerald green. Looking far to the horizon, the water changed color to a magnificent deep sapphire blue. The sky was so clear you could see into Heaven. The sunset was radiantly crimson red. The mountains in the backdrop were majestic, lustrous green with mist hovering on the peaks. Coconut trees, mangroves, and scarlet red and bright yellow tropical flowers blanketed the entire island. Kauai is a beautiful paradise. Johnny Depp, Orlando Bloom, and the filming crew were shooting their third episode of *Pirates of the Caribbean* on the beach and in the wet cave. We drove on a rustic wooden road along the bay to the Blue Dolphin restaurant where we ate the best sushi we had ever tasted. We hiked the mountain, picnicked, and looked down to the beach where they were making the movie.

Kauai Island really was beautiful. You might imagine that people there don't need the Lord. But they do. People there need to be saved just as much as anyone else. Sometimes Christian people have a false perception that a missionary ought to go only to countries such as

Africa or Cambodia, not Hawaii. Well, people in Hawaii need the Lord too. People there need to be saved as much as people on the Women's Island in Cambodia.

While we were on our vacation in Kauai, Rachel and I led a French-Belgian businessman to the Lord. The way we met this man was extremely unusual. What are the chances of a French-speaking Cambodian-American man meeting a French-Belgian living in Kauai? The chance is very probable when the Lord is in it. Only the Lord can divinely plan a meeting like this. God is always at work for His purpose and His glory. We just have to find Him and join Him. And when we do, our life will be changed and blessed.

On Sunday Rachel and I went to church. Early in the morning I opened the Kauai Yellow Pages, thumbing through looking for a church to attend. I just picked one out of the many churches listed. We arrived early to an elementary school. In the yard there was a sign, "Church Meeting This Sunday." The church service was being held in the breezeway between the two school buildings. The mountain was in the background. After the service, two women introduced themselves to us. They were a mother and daughter in their sixties and forties, respectively. We told them that we were missionaries and we were here on vacation. The women visited with Rachel while I stood waiting. I don't know what all they said, but I heard the daughter say, "Please pray for my husband's salvation." We told them that we would and said goodbye.

After shopping one afternoon, Rachel and I stopped at a restaurant to catch a bite. There are many places to eat on the island, but it just happened that we chose the same place as the two women we had met at church. Was this a coincidence? I don't think so. They saw us, came to our table, and made some recommendations. By this time we knew the daughter's name was Hannah and she was from the Philippines. She said her husband owned the restaurant. Before they left, Hannah again asked us to pray for her husband's salvation. We told her that we would.

Can you believe that the next day we met the same two women again at the shopping mall? The entire week, we did not meet anyone else from the church but these two women. I sat on the bench and waited while Rachel talked with them. Hannah was in tears. She wept and talked at the same time.

"Peter is a good man. I have been praying for him for more than ten years, but he doesn't want to get saved. What do I need to do? What do you tell a person when he thinks he is good enough? Please pray for him. I don't want him to die and go to Hell."

Rachel gave me the look, "Bong, can we have them over for dinner at our condo?"

She had caught me off guard, "We are on vacation darling, and we don't have much time," I contested.

"Let's put feet to our prayer. Just one evening, please? We can spare an evening. Look, I will cook and you can share our faith with Peter," Rachel pleaded.

"All right, let's do it. We are flying out on Saturday, you know. So let's have them over on Thursday evening," I reluctantly agreed with Rachel, who then spoke with Hannah.

"We would love to have you and Peter over to our place for dinner. My husband can talk with Peter about the Lord. And we can pray. What about Thursday at 5:30 p.m.?"

"I am not sure. Peter is camping with the Boy Scouts on the mountain with our son. They are not coming down until Thursday afternoon," Hannah hesitated.

"You have asked us to pray for your husband's salvation. We want to meet with him in person. Come if you can. Here is my phone number and address." Rachel wrote on a piece of paper and handed it to her.

On Thursday, Rachel and I went deep sea fishing during the day. The sea was rough and I got very sick, but we managed to cook and clean preparing for our guests. The clock on the microwave showed 6:00 p.m. already and there was no sign of our guests anywhere. I was looking for their arrival every few minutes. Feeling really disappointed, I told Rachel, "Let's eat. They are not coming." Just as soon as we started to sit down, the doorbell rang. Peter and Hannah had showed up.

For two hours we visited and ate dinner. We watched the beautiful sunset over Hanalei Bay. I enjoyed speaking my Okie-French with Peter.

Peter was seeking the Lord. Recently he had lost his best friend, who was also his business partner, to cancer. "Losing my best friend causes me to think about my priorities." Peter spoke with a French accent. Obviously, the Lord had been dealing with him about his eternal destiny, and He sent Rachel and me to help. That evening Peter repented of his sin, bowed his head, prayed the sinner's prayer, and asked Jesus to be his Lord and Saviour. Hannah and Peter cried soberly. Wiping the tears from his eyes, Peter said, "Today my destiny has been changed."

Peter's life was changed and God added more joy for Rachel and me. On that evening, Peter received the greatest gift given to man which cannot be bought with any price.

What a great and magnificent God we serve. He divinely orchestrates everything according to His purpose. He led a couple from the "Killing Fields," brought them to Oklahoma, then took them to Kauai for a vacation, just to lead one man to Himself. I am so glad that my wife was caring enough to take time even during our anniversary to minister to people in need. What a memorable vacation we had. It was such a joy seeing Peter coming to know Christ.

On that island, I learned an important lesson. The lesson is that no one really cares how much you know, but only how much you really care. Jesus' second greatest commandment is for us to love our neighbors as ourselves. From external appearances, Peter looked like he had it all—wealth, health, and family. However, down deep in his heart he was spiritually bankrupt. He knew that he needed God to fill the void. Peter's salvation in Kauai's paradise is as sweet as salvation for a fisherman on the Yellowstone River in Montana, and as sweet as salvation for a sex slave in Cambodia.

What if every Christian in the world decided to care for the lost? What if each one of us could just reach one lost soul for the Lord because we care?

Before he left for Latvia on a mission trip, my friend Jonathan Dougherty wrote this on a card: "Charles Spurgeon says, Every Christian is either a missionary or an imposter." The psalmist says that true Christians ". . . give thanks unto the LORD; call upon his name: make known his deeds among the people. Sing unto him, sing psalms unto him: talk ye of all his wondrous works" (Psalms 105:1–2).

A missionary friend told me a story about an eye surgeon who went to the mission field in a third world country. The surgeon performed a delicate eye surgery on a blind man. The surgery was successful, and the blind man was able to see for the first time in his life. Shortly after the surgery, the man with new sight disappeared. Everyone wondered where he was. They looked for him everywhere, but they could not find him. Three days later the man with new sight appeared with a long rope in his hand leading many other blind people behind him. He had brought them to the surgeon who had given him his sight.

Just like the man with the new sight, that's how it ought to be with us Christians. We should be going around gathering lost people and bringing them to Jesus. We care and love people because we know what it is like to be lost and without hope. We tell others because we love God and we care! Wouldn't you go to help if you knew that there was a helpless baby trapped in the bottom of a well?

Over twenty years ago, an eighteen-month–old baby girl fell into an eight-inch pipe in Midland, Texas. Baby Jessica, as she became known, was trapped in that well for fifty-nine hours. Twenty-two feet down in the hole, Baby Jessica was wedged in the steel pipe. Rescuers piped fresh air and heat down to her while they labored nonstop to rescue her. The whole country held their breath. News about Baby Jessica was everywhere, from television, to radio, to newspapers. The rescue operation was flooded with resources and much prayer without ceasing. No resource was spared to rescue this helpless baby. When Baby Jessica was finally pulled out of that eight-inch opening, a filthy but alert eighteen-month-old girl was wrapped in gauze and strapped to a backboard. Rescuers cheered and church bells rang out, letting all know that the ordeal was over. The family was later honored at a reception sponsored by the White House with President George H. W. Bush, and First Lady Barbara Bush.

Ten years later, a Pew Research Center project showed that only the death of Princess Diana drew more worldwide media coverage than Jessica's rescue. Twenty years later, in an interview, Baby Jessica, now a grown woman and married with a baby of her own, said this about her rescuers: "I explain to myself that I believe that people cared so much because they would hope that somebody would care that much about them."

Chapter 21

To Be a 'Miss-she-ary'.

When Mollina was just a little girl and was not yet able to speak clearly, she used to tell me, "Daddy, when I grow up, I want to be a miss-she-ary." Not understanding what she was saying, I asked her to explain what she meant. "You know, people who go to another country to tell others about Jesus," Mollina explained what she understood to be the answer for the hopelessness of the world.

Mollina grew up too fast. During her last year of high school, when she was about seventeen years old, Mollina went to Cambodia to serve as a missionary teaching English and Bible studies in one of the remote villages. Letting our daughter go to a country where we knew it to be unsafe required a lot of courage and faith in God. It was the most difficult decision we had ever made in our lives, but we trusted God with her.

Mollina went to live for six months among the Cambodian people in a very a remote and primitive village which had no modern conveniences such as electricity or running water. She bathed with water from a pond. She gathered firewood from a forest for her cooking, and she gathered vegetables and fruit from the fields for food.

At first, Mollina began classes underneath the shade of a bamboo bush. Her students were all poor village children who had no access to education. They all desired to get an education, but they couldn't afford it. These children had to delicately balance their lives between daily chores and going to school. The children had to get up extremely early, before the sunrise, to help their parents work in the field. They had to hurriedly complete all their daily chores before they could go to class.

One of the students was a little boy named Chou. He was named for the sad, sour expression he wore on his face. Chou was the youngest of four children in his family. He was severely malnourished to the point that his growth was stunted. His parents were extremely poor and they blamed Chou for their misfortune. They treated him like he was the biggest mistake of their lives. Chou's face was usually soiled and his clothes were dirty and tattered. When the other children were bubbly and smiling in Mollina's class, Chou was always standing at a distance with a frown on his face. However, Chou was always there in class.

As a reward to her students, Mollina would give special treats like sweet mango, coconut, cookies, and toys. She would give extra to Chou, trying to make him feel special. However, Chou remained reserved and didn't respond in spite of her efforts.

"Chou, can you smile for me?" Mollina constantly asked, but Chou would tuck his chin and look down.

"Chou, I love you, and so does Jesus." Mollina said that to him every day.

Summers in Cambodia can get unbearably hot and humid, especially for an American teenage girl who is used to staying in an air conditioned house. Noticing Mollina's difficulty in coping with the heat, a few men in the village got together to build her a new classroom. Her beautiful classroom was a thatched roof gazebo suspended on stilts in the pond. The cool breeze from the water made it more comfortable for Mollina, and this was where she continued to hold her classes until she returned home.

While her new classroom gave Mollina much more comfort, there were other elements that brought her fear and challenge. Remember, Cambodia is infested with poisonous snakes. One day a cobra was found inside Mollina's hut, and two others were found outside near her hut. One day, when Mollina saw a cobra next to her hut she screamed really loud for help. A dog came running to her rescue, barking and attacking the vicious snake, but the cobra sprayed its venomous spit into the dog's eyes. The dog went blind and the snake vanished into the woods. Being extremely frightened, Mollina called me asking for instructions on how to kill a cobra. I instructed her to stay away from the area until I got there in the next few days. When I got there, I cut a big long stick from a tree and went hunting for the cobra. I walked all over the land, but I couldn't find it. It must have slithered away deep into the woods.

The hot, humid weather was another challenge for Mollina, but it was something she could cope with. To help her stay comfortable in the heat, Mollina frequently bathed at a pond. When she went bathing, she would also take her dirty clothes with her to wash. One time Chou accompanied Mollina, helping her to carry her laundry basket to the pond. Mollina talked and teased Chou as they walked together. After spending almost six months there with him, Chou cracked his first smile for Mollina. "It was beautiful and worth it all to see Chou smile."

Mollina told this story in her high school graduation speech. With tears in her eyes, Mollina continued, "When I was little girl I used to tell my daddy that I was going to be a miss-she-ary when I grew up. I wasn't very sure then, but after spending six months in Cambodia I have made up my mind. I will go to college and become a missionary dentist. I want to help people to have the joy of smiling for Jesus."

Rachel and I are very proud of our daughter's decision. God is so gracious and amazing. Not only did He save my wife and me from the Killing Fields, now He has given our family the privilege to return to do His work.

The Word of God clearly demonstrates God's goodness in this way, "Now unto him that is able to do exceeding abundantly above all that we ask or think, according to the power that worketh in us,

Unto him be glory in the church by Christ Jesus throughout all ages, world without end. Amen" (Ephesians 3:20–21).

Since our return to Cambodia, we have focused on evangelism, discipleship, partnership with the house church pastors, assisting the sick and the poor, and educating the next generation. In other words, we come along with a house church pastor to assist him spreading the gospel, discipling new believers, acquiring land to build a house church, distributing medicine to the sick, digging water wells, and teaching young people English from the Bible. We have always had many people willing to come with us, but we never had anyone who chose to stay on for a long term living in the village and teaching English and the Bible. On several occasions people came to me saying that they were very interested in it, but none followed through.

Our house church pastor in Cambodia pleaded with us to send an English teacher. Teaching English from the Bible in the village is the most needed and effective tool to reach young people for Christ. Many of them are very poor and can't afford to pay for English lessons which are usually being taught in the city. Young people have so much desire to better themselves, and they believe that learning the English language will give them an advantage in life.

You can make a big difference in people's lives by purchasing this book.

Because of the war in Cambodia many women and children have been left homeless and destitute. Many of them have been subjected to sex slavery and human trafficking. Without any help, these desperate people would remain hopeless in the abyss of their misery. We can help by giving them a place to call home. We buy small lots and build a small hut big enough to shelter widows and children in the villages. This project requires minimum cost and upkeep. The widows take care of the children and the home. These homes are also used for worship-house churches.

Next to the house church there is usually a garden and water well. Widows and orphans in Cambodia can have food and clean water to drink. In the summer, water is very scarce. Villagers have to walk a long way in the hot, blistering sun to carry water from a puddle far away from their home. This water can often be infested with parasites and animal waste. No wonder people often get very sick; some of the children die very young. By buying this book you are helping the widows and the children with the gift of clean water. Your support will go to dig water wells next to one of the house churches in a village.

Right now we have many believers meeting under the mango trees. We need more house churches and water wells.

We hope to build a place called "House of Joy." Rachel and I have already purchased forty acres of land in the mountains of Cambodia for this. We need funds to build House of Joy. We hope to sell enough books for this needy project. At House of Joy, pastors and their spouses can come to "refuel" their tanks spiritually, emotionally, and physically. These pastors and wives are weary and worn out from overwork and not enough rest. They have served God tirelessly without getting paid. Many pastors shepherd several house churches. The road can be long, hot, and dusty, or it can be wet, cold, and rainy. These pastors ride scooters long hours to get there. Sometimes they run out of gas or food.

These pastors often get exhausted and sick. Pastor Mony was hospitalized for a week because he couldn't breathe. Too much dust from the road congested his lungs. One pastor was almost killed by a king cobra when he ran over the back of the snake with his scooter. The snake tried to bite him, but instead its fang punctured the rear tire. Pastor Khan has club feet. He can barely walk, but that doesn't stop him. He rides his scooter to minister in house churches in the woods. Like Pastor Mony, who cleans toilets for a living, most of these pastors are rice farmers. They have to work long hours in the field to support themselves. They plow the field. They plant and reap the crop.

House of Joy will be a resting place for pastors and their wives. They can come and stay a few weeks for free. These pastors and their wives have never had such a place before. We hope to build it in the near future as soon as funds are available. You can make a difference in the lives of people in Cambodia by buying this book and by recommending it to a friend or family member.

We hope and pray that we will raise the financial support needed by selling many copies of this book. With the resources from selling this book we can help build more house churches, help shelter many widows and orphans, dig more water wells, and build House of Joy for pastors and their spouses to refuel themselves.

Our goal is to evangelize and disciple the Cambodian people for Jesus by partnering with the house church pastors. Together we will reach the lost by proclaiming the gospel. We will disciple the believers through building relationships and Bible teaching. We will help the sick, and assist with the poor, but most of all, we will love them like Jesus would.

Your contribution will go toward one of the three mission projects in Cambodia:

1. Building house churches.
2. Digging water wells.
3. Building a place called House of Joy for pastors and their spouses.

Please send your tax-deductible contribution to:

Central Missionary Clearing House
c/o Dr. Heng Lim
P. O. Box 219228
Houston, TX 77218

About The Author

 **DR. HENG LIM** lives in the Tulsa area of Oklahoma with his wife and two daughters. He and his family are members of the First Baptist Church of Owasso, where he leads the young married class. Dr. Lim has a dental practice in Owasso where he focuses on neuromuscular dentistry, dental implants, reconstruction, and TMJ. People have come to him from all over America for treatment of migraine headaches, and neck and facial pains. Because of Dr. Lim's passion to share the love of God, he and his family have led numerous mission trips to Cambodia.